World Geography Puzzles:
Countries of the World

Editor: Mary Dieterich
Proofreaders: Cindy Neisen and Margaret Brown

COPYRIGHT © 2018 Mark Twain Media, Inc.

ISBN 978-1-62223-692-3

Printing No. CD-405015

Mark Twain Media, Inc., Publishers
Distributed by Carson-Dellosa Publishing LLC

The purchase of this book entitles the buyer to reproduce the student pages for classroom use only. Other permissions may be obtained by writing Mark Twain Media, Inc., Publishers.

All rights reserved. Printed in the United States of America.

Visit us at www.carsondellosa.com

Table of Contents

Canada	1
Mexico	3
Panama	5
Brazil	7
Chile	9
Sweden	11
United Kingdom	13
France	15
Croatia	17
Italy	19
Russia	21
Egypt	23
Nigeria	25
Zambia	27
South Africa	29
Iraq	31
India	33
China	35
Japan	37
Australia	39
Answer Keys	41
Bibliography	44
Photo Credits	46

Introduction

World Geography Puzzles: Countries of the World provides students with a variety of fun and challenging puzzles designed to reinforce geography concepts, such as location, place, human-environment interaction, movement, and regions. The units present information about selected countries and then give students an opportunity to reinforce that knowledge by completing crosswords, word searches, hidden messages, and various other types of puzzles. These activities will give students a chance to review what they have been learning in their social studies classes.

Whether used as an additional lesson while studying a certain country or geography concept or as a stand-alone activity, students will enjoy learning about the countries of the world while completing these fun puzzle units.

CANADA

Canada Quick Facts

Official Name: Canada
Total area: 9,984,670 sq km
Population: 35,362,905 (July 2016 est.)
GDP: $1.674 trillion (2016 est.)
Government: parliamentary democracy under a constitutional monarchy
Capital: Ottawa
Motto: "from sea to sea"

Canada is located in the Northern and Western Hemispheres, just north of the United States. It is the second-largest country in the world in land area. It also has the longest coastline in the world, as it is surrounded on three sides by the Atlantic Ocean, Arctic Ocean, and Pacific Ocean. Its land border with the United States is the longest international border in the world.

The name Canada comes from the Huron-Iroquois word *Kanata,* meaning "village." This referred to the settlement where Quebec City is now. Since much of Canada is located north of 60° North latitude where conditions are harsh, most of the population lives in the southern part of Canada within 160 km (100 mi.) of the southern border.

Canadian Parliament Building Near the Ottawa River

The nation of Canada has ten provinces and three territories. The provinces of Central Canada are Quebec and Ontario. More than half of Canada's population lives in these provinces. The capital city Ottawa is in Ontario. This is where most of the commerce, industry, and manufacturing take place. On the south, these provinces border the Great Lakes and the St. Lawrence River. Hudson Bay is on their northern borders.

The Maritime Provinces all border the Atlantic Ocean. These are Newfoundland and Labrador, Prince Edward Island, Nova Scotia, and New Brunswick. These island and peninsular provinces are closely connected to the sea, and the earliest trade and settlement in Canada occurred there. The region is known for its fishing and farming.

The Prairie Provinces of Manitoba, Saskatchewan, and Alberta are known for their fertile farmland and rich energy resources. The farms here produce most of Canada's grain, beef, and other agricultural products. Oil and gas production, mining, and hydroelectric power generation are concentrated here on the vast plains of this region.

British Columbia is the only province in the Pacific or West Coast Region. It borders the continental United States on the south and shares a long border with Alaska on the west up to 60°N. The province includes Vancouver Island and many other islands on the west coast. The region is known for forestry, mining, shipping, and fishing. This is a mountainous province that includes the Canadian Rockies and the Coast Mountains.

The Northern Territories of Nunavut, Northwest Territories, and Yukon Territory are sparsely populated. Many of the people are of native Inuit descent. This region is sometimes called "the land of the midnight sun" because during the peak of summer there can be 24-hour daylight. The region also has a period of 24-hour darkness in the winter. The region borders the Arctic Ocean on the north, and Yukon Territory borders Alaska on the west. Mining, hunting, fishing, and trapping are the major industries.

Symbols of Canada include the maple leaf and the beaver. Canada has long been a major producer of maple syrup, and the beaver goes back to the early fur trade. Canada Day is July 1st. It celebrates the Constitution Act of 1867, which created Canada as a self-governing dominion of the British Empire. The head of government is the prime minister, and the head of state is the ruling monarch of the United Kingdom.

Canada Crossword Puzzle

Directions: Use the clues below to complete the puzzle about Canada.

Across

6. The Canadian ____ run through British Columbia.
7. Canada shares the longest international border in the world with the ____ ____.
9. The Northern Territories are called "the land of the ____ ____."
10. The ____ ____ is a symbol of Canada found on its flag.
11. The ____ Territory shares a border with Alaska.
13. One of the Prairie Provinces where agriculture and oil are important
14. The ruling monarch of the United Kingdom is the head of ____.
15. Canada means "____."

Down

1. Vancouver Island belongs to the province of ____ ____.
2. The ____ Provinces all border the Atlantic Ocean.
3. Large body of water on the northern borders of Quebec and Ontario (two words)
4. The ____ ____ are on the southern borders of Quebec and Ontario.
5. The head of the Canadian government is the ____ ____.
8. Capital of Canada
12. Most people in Nunavut are of ____ descent.

MEXICO

Mexico Quick Facts

Official Name: United Mexican States
Total area: 1,964,375 sq km
Population: 123,166,749 (July 2016 est.)
GDP: $2.307 trillion (2016 est.)
Government: federal presidential republic
Capital: Mexico City
Motto: no official motto

Mexico consists of 31 states and the federal district of Mexico City. The national Independence Day holiday is on September 16. This celebrates the country declaring its independence from Spain in 1810. The president is the head of government and the chief of state. Presidential elections are held every six years. The two-house legislature consists of the Senate and the Chamber of Deputies. Mexico's Supreme Court of Justice has 11 justices and one chief justice. Symbols of Mexico include the golden eagle and the national colors of green, white, and red. These are all shown on the Mexican flag.

The geography of Mexico varies greatly. There are deserts, canyons, plateaus, mountains, tropical forests, and beaches. It bridges the gap between the more temperate North American climate and the more tropical climate of Central America. Mexico shares its northern border with the United States. The Rio Grande forms the border between Mexico and Texas. The Gulf of Mexico is on the eastern border of Mexico, and the Pacific Ocean is on the western border. On the southeast, Mexico borders Guatemala and Belize.

Mountains are a major feature of Mexico's landscape. The Sierra Madre Oriental is the mountain range in the eastern part of the country. The Sierra Madre Occidental runs along the western part of the country from the northern border to the south where it runs into the Sierra Madre del Sur range. Copper Canyon, which is actually a complex of canyons formed by six different rivers, is located in the Occidental range. It is the deepest canyon in North America, with depths up to 1,870 m (6,135 ft). The highest point in Mexico is Pico de Orizaba, a volcanic mountain that is 5,610 m (18,406 ft) tall. Many of Mexico's peaks are volcanoes, and many of them are still active.

Palace of Fine Arts in Mexico City

Mexico has beautiful beaches along the Baha Peninsula, the Pacific Coast, and the Gulf of Mexico. The warm tropical waters and beautiful scenery have provided the perfect place for resort towns. Vacationers from all over the world enjoy spending time in resorts in cities like Cabo San Lucas, Puerto Vallarta, Acapulco, and Cancun.

Deserts and shrublands cover most of the Central Mexican Plateau. It is in the northern and central region of Mexico. This region is at an average of 1,825 m (5,988 ft) above sea level. The northern part of the plateau is dry and must be irrigated for farming. Most of the people of Mexico live in the southern plateau region, which receives more rain and has fertile soil. Most of the major cities, including Mexico City, are located here.

Crops produced in Mexico for export include sugar, coffee, fruits, and vegetables. Mexico has large forest reserves, but the forests are in danger of being cut for expansion of farmland or mining operations. Mexico has large mineral deposits, including silver, copper, salt, iron, zinc, mercury, and gold. Petroleum is the most valuable mineral resource in the country. Most of the oil reserves are found in the southeastern part of the country and offshore in the Gulf of Mexico.

World Geography Puzzles: Countries of the World   Mexico

Name: _____ Date: _____

MEXICO HIDDEN MESSAGE PUZZLE

Directions: Use the clues below to fill in the blanks at the right. When you are finished, unscramble the letters in the circled blanks and write them in the blanks to complete the hidden message at the bottom of the page.

1. Mexicans celebrate independence from ____ on September 16.   _Ⓢ_ _ _ _

2. The ____ ____ forms the border between Mexico and Texas.   _ _Ⓞ_ _ _ _ _ _ _

3. Mexico's government is a federal presidential ____.   _ _ _ _ _Ⓒ_ _

4. The Sierra Madre ____ are on the eastern part of Mexico.   Ⓞ_ _ _ _ _ _ _ _

5. The Sierra Madre ____ are on the western side of Mexico.   _ _Ⓒ_ _ _ _ _ _ _

6. The Central Mexican Plateau is almost 6,000 feet above ____ ____.   _ _ _ _ _Ⓐ_ _

7. Beautiful beaches are the highlight of resort towns like ____.   Ⓐ_ _ _ _ _ _ _ _

8. Most of the major cities are in the southern part of the Central Mexican ____.   _ _ _Ⓣ_ _ _

9. Oil reserves are mostly found ____ in the Gulf of Mexico.   _ _ _ _ _ _ _

10. Copper ____ is the deepest in North America.   _ _ _ _Ⓝ_

Hidden Message: Many of Mexico's mountain peaks are _ _ _ _ _ _ _ _ _ _.

CD-405015 ©Mark Twain Media, Inc., Publishers   4

PANAMA

Panama Quick Facts

Official Name: Republic of Panama
Total area: 75,420 sq km
Population: 3,705,246 (July 2016 est.)
GDP: $93.12 billion (2016 est.)
Government: presidential republic
Capital: Panama City
Motto: For the Benefit of the World

The country of Panama has a unique place in world geography. It is located at the narrowest part of the land that connects North America and South America. This geographic feature is called the Isthmus of Panama. At the narrowest, it is about 60 km (37 mi.) wide.

This area was considered the most likely spot to build a canal that could connect the Caribbean Sea with the Pacific Ocean. Ships could avoid the long trip around South America and save 12,669 km (7,872 mi.) if the canal could be built. The French were the first to try to build a canal, but their effort failed. The United States struck a deal with Panama by backing their move for independence from Colombia on November 3, 1903. The United States paid $10 million and continued yearly payments of $250,000. In return, the United States received control of a 10-mile-wide strip of land, known as the Panama Canal Zone.

The U.S. Army Corps of Engineers constructed the canal between 1904 and 1914. In addition to the challenges of digging through the terrain, thousands of workers died from mosquito-born illnesses, such as malaria and yellow fever. The first ship steamed through the Panama Canal on August 15, 1914. By the late twentieth century, the United States began transferring control of the Panama Canal back to Panama. In 1999, full control of the canal, the Canal Zone, and U.S. bases was turned over to Panama.

The major port cities in Panama are Cristóbal and Colón on the Caribbean coast and Balboa on the Pacific side. There are numerous islands in the Caribbean and the Pacific that belong to Panama. Two of the largest are the Isla del Rey and the Isla de Coiba. Most of Panama's rivers are unnavigable. The Rio Chepo and Rio Chagres have been dammed to produce hydroelectric power. Gatun Lake, a major part of the Panama Canal, and Alajuela Lake were filled with water from the Rio Chagres. The Rio Tuira is the only Panamanian river that large vessels can navigate.

Panama has a tropical climate. The temperatures do not vary much, with daytime dry-season temperatures of about 24°C to 29°C (75°F to 84°F). Almost all the rain comes during the rainy season from April to December. Rainfall is heavier on the Caribbean side than on the Pacific side. Average rainfall varies by region, with some receiving less than 1.3 m (51 in) and others receiving more than 3 m (118 in) per year. The capital city of Panama City gets about half the rainfall of the city of Colón.

The mountain range of the continental divide that stretches from the border with Costa Rica to the canal is called the Cordillera Central. The highest point at 3,474 m (11,397 ft) is an ancient volcano named Volcan Baru. About 40 percent of the country is covered in tropical rain forest. There are small farms producing corn, beans, and tubers for local use. Expansion of farms and development continues to threaten the rain forest. Most of the people live in the central part of the country near the Canal Zone. The Darien province in the eastern part of the country, which borders Colombia, is sparsely populated. It features rain forests, rivers, swampy lowlands, and high mountains.

World Geography Puzzles: Countries of the World   Panama

Name: _____   Date: _____

PANAMA LAST LETTER/FIRST LETTER PUZZLE

Directions: Use the clues below to help you fill in the last letter/first letter puzzle. The last letter of one word will be the first letter of the next word. The words will go down one column and up the next in a continuous line. Letters have been placed in the puzzle to help you.

1. The _____ of Panama is the narrow part of the land that connects North and South America.
2. With a canal through Panama, ships could avoid the long trip around _____ America.
3. Some of Panama's rivers are dammed to produce _____ power.
4. Panama declared its independence from _____ on November 3, 1903.
5. The U.S. _____ Corps of Engineers constructed the Panama Canal.
6. _____ _____ and other diseases killed thousands of workers.
7. Water from the _____ _____ filled Gatun Lake.
8. The first _____ went through the Panama Canal on August 15, 1914.
9. _____ City, the capital, gets about half the rainfall of Colón.
10. The highest point in Panama is an _____ volcano named Volcan Baru.
11. The United States began _____ control of the Panama Canal back to Panama.
12. _____ Lake is a major part of the Panama Canal.
13. Large vessels can _____ the Rio Tuira.
14. The French _____ to build a canal failed.
15. By the end of the _____ century, full control of the Panama Canal was turned over to Panama.

CD-405015 ©Mark Twain Media, Inc., Publishers   6

BRAZIL

Brazil Quick Facts

Official Name: Federative Republic of Brazil
Total area: 8,515,770 sq km
Population: 205,823,665 (July 2016 est.)
GDP: $3.135 trillion (2016 est.)
Government: federal presidential republic
Capital: Brasilia
Motto: Order and Progress

Brazil is the largest country in South America and the fifth largest country in the world. It was a colony of Portugal, and Portuguese is still the most widely spoken language. Brazil declared its independence from Portugal in 1822, and September 7 is celebrated as Independence Day.

The president is both the head of the government and the chief of state. The president is elected by popular vote for a single four-year term. There are 26 states and one federal district. The legislature is called the National Congress. It is composed of the Federal Senate and the Chamber of Deputies. The Supreme Federal Court consists of 11 justices.

Brazil is known for its vast rain forests and river systems. The Amazon rain forest accounts for about half of the world's rain forests. It contains an estimated one-third of all the known animal species in the world. Rain forests cover about 60 percent of Brazil.

Most of the rain forest area is located in the Amazon River Basin. The Amazon River flows through the northern half of Brazil. Where the Amazon flows into the Atlantic Ocean, the rate of discharge is 209,000 cubic meters (55,212,000 U.S. gallons) of water per second. The Amazon River Basin generally experiences flooding from November to June. This is mainly due to the rainy seasons in the Andes Mountains of Ecuador and Peru.

Federal Senate of Brazil

The climate of the Amazon Rain Forest is warm, rainy, and humid. Temperatures in the city of Manaus average from 32°C (upper 80s F) in September to 24°C (mid-70s F) in April. Other areas of Brazil can be dry. Brazil has five different ecosystems: the tropical rain forest, the Pantanal (a tropical wetland), the Cerrado (a tropical savanna), the Mata Atlantica (the Atlantic forest), and the pampas (fertile plains).

The Brazilian Highlands or Brazilian Plateau covers most of the central, eastern, and southern parts of Brazil. The area is generally under 1,220 m (4,000 ft) above sea level. The highest peak in Brazil is Pico da Neblina at 2,995 m (9,827 ft). It is located in northwestern Brazil, right next to the border with Venezuela.

Agriculture is an important part of Brazil's economy. Most of the country's grains, sugarcane, and oilseeds are grown in southern Brazil. Central Brazil has recently seen an increase in agriculture with new techniques for growing soybeans and other crops. Cattle are raised mainly in central Brazil, as well. In northeast Brazil, the major crops are cocoa, tropical fruits, and forest products. Many families in this area grow food for their own survival. Deforestation occurs as the rain forest is cleared to provide new land for farming. However, after a few years of farming, the land becomes less fertile.

Brazil is also rich in mineral resources. Bauxite, gold, iron ore, manganese, nickel, uranium, and petroleum are plentiful. In fact, the yellow on the Brazilian flag represents gold and other minerals and the green represents the forests.

World Geography Puzzles: Countries of the World   Brazil

Name: _____   Date: _____

BRAZIL CODED PUZZLE

Directions: Use the decoder key to fill in the blanks for each statement below.

A	B	C	D	E	F	G	H	I	J	K	L	M	N	O	P	Q	R	S	T	U	V	W	X	Y	Z
13	12	11	10	9	8	7	6	5	4	3	2	1	26	25	24	23	22	21	20	19	18	17	16	15	14

1. The capital of Brazil is __ __ __ __ __ __ __ __.
   12 22 13 21 5 2 5 13

2. Brazil declared its independence from __ __ __ __ __ __ __ __ on September 7, 1822.
   24 25 22 20 19 7 13 2

3. The __ __ __ __ __ __ __ __ __ __ __ is called the National Congress.
   2 9 7 5 21 2 13 20 19 22 9

4. The Amazon __ __ __ __ __ __ __ __ __ __ contains about
   22 13 5 26   8 25 22 9 21 20
   one-third of all the known animal species in the world.

5. Flooding in the __ __ __ __ __ __ River Basin occurs from November to June.
   13 1 13 14 25 26

6. The __ __ __ __ __ __ __ __ is a tropical wetland ecosystem.
   24 13 26 20 13 26 13 2

7. The Brazilian __ __ __ __ __ __ __ __ feature hills generally
   6 5 7 6 2 13 26 10 21
   lower than 1,220 meters high.

8. Brazil's highest peak, Pico da Neblina, is located along the border
   with __ __ __ __ __ __ __ __.
   18 9 26 9 14 19 9 2 13

9. In central Brazil, new techniques for growing __ __ __ __ __ __ __ __ and other crops
   21 25 15 12 9 13 26 21
   have led to an increase in agriculture.

10. __ __ __ __ __ __ __ is one of the mineral resources of Brazil.
    19 22 13 26 5 19 1

Bonus: __ __ __ __ __ and __ __ __ __ __ __ __ are the only two South American countries
11 6 5 2 9   9 11 19 13 10 25 22
that do not border Brazil.

CD-405015 ©Mark Twain Media, Inc., Publishers   8

CHILE

Chile Quick Facts

Official Name: Republic of Chile
Total area: 8,515,770 sq km
Population: 17,650,114 (July 2016 est.)
GDP: $436.1 billion (2016 est.)
Government: presidential republic
Capital: Santiago
Motto: By right or by might

Chile is located on the western and southern edge of South America. It is a narrow country with the high, rugged Andes Mountains on the east and the Pacific Ocean on the west. Most of the country is covered in mountains, deep valleys, and high plateaus.

The Central Valley is where most of the people live. It extends roughly from the capital Santiago south to Concepción. This is where most of the country's agriculture takes place. In the northern part of the valley there are vineyards and large farms. Fruits, vegetables, grains, beef, and poultry are the major agricultural products. In the southern part, there are forests and lakes.

Chile's terrain and geographical location present some difficulties for its people. The Andes Mountains contain over 600 volcanoes within Chile's borders, and many of them are active. There is also a risk of tsunamis along the coast. Earthquake activity is common in Chile. Some of the greatest magnitude earthquakes ever recorded have occurred in Chile. When earthquakes occur in Chile or off its shores, tsunami waves hit the coast of Chile very quickly and for a sustained period of time. This can cause great damage and loss of life. However, the waves also travel across the Pacific Ocean and cause death and destruction as they come ashore in places like Hawaii, Japan, and the Asian mainland.

In northern Chile, the Atacama Desert is one of the driest places on Earth. It is a high plateau between the Chilean Coastal Range and the Andes Mountains. The land is covered with salt basins and lava flows. Some parts of this desert may have never seen rain. The area is a rich source of copper, one of Chile's major exports.

Copper Mine in Chile

Easter Island is a territory of Chile. The island is famous for its mysterious stone statues called moai. It is located 3,700 km (2,300 mi.) off the west coast of Chile in the Pacific Ocean.

In the south, there are thousands of mountainous islands that form archipelagos (chains of islands). The coastline is full of winding channels and fjords. There are huge ice fields in the Patagonian region. Glaciers move out away from the ice fields. Some move toward glacial lakes to the east, and some move toward fjords that empty into the Pacific on the west. The southernmost headland in South America is at Cape Horn on Hornos Island. This is part of the archipelago of Tierra del Fuego. The name means "Land of Fire" and may refer to the bonfires of the natives seen by early explorers.

The Incas moved into northern Chile in the fifteenth century. They made their way into the Central Valley until they met the Mapuche who were living in the region. The Inca army was unable to defeat the Mapuche, so they stayed north of the Lake District. The Spanish moved into the region in the early 1500s and were able to defeat the Incas. However, the Spanish were never able to remove the Mapuche from the area. They remained in control of their territory in the Lake District until settlers gradually pushed them out in the mid-1800s.

The country declared its independence from Spain on September 18, 1810. However, there were seven years of war before Chile was granted independence in 1817. Today, Chile has a stable government and one of the strongest economies in South America.

World Geography Puzzles: Countries of the World   Chile

Name: _____   Date: _____

CHILE WORD SEARCH PUZZLE

Directions: Use the clues below to determine the words associated with Chile that are in the puzzle. Write the words on the lines provided and find and circle them in the word search puzzle.

```
B  X  U  O  A  E  V  S  E  O  N  A  C  L  O  V
P  Q  P  O  A  R  Q  V  N  R  O  H  E  P  A  C
D  A  Q  T  G  R  W  T  H  Z  P  R  Q  V  V  G
I  L  C  Y  D  Y  C  T  D  I  N  C  A  S  I  I
V  A  A  I  E  N  D  H  I  D  I  P  L  J  N  I
G  O  U  V  F  L  A  Y  I  T  E  A  T  G  E  E
M  N  T  Q  A  I  L  L  N  P  S  S  Y  G  Y  B
C  A  S  H  M  F  C  A  S  F  E  W  K  I  A  O
O  I  U  N  B  A  L  O  V  I  Z  L  A  Q  R  W
G  N  N  S  Y  H  P  O  C  L  R  S  A  U  D  F
A  O  A  E  X  Y  I  U  W  E  A  E  D  G  S  P
I  G  M  D  K  A  Y  J  C  S  A  R  T  G  O  Q
T  A  I  N  V  J  N  J  D  H  W  N  T  S  B  L
N  T  S  A  X  Z  R  N  X  L  E  A  T  N  A  S
A  A  A  I  S  J  F  T  S  H  R  S  Y  R  E  E
S  P  A  T  A  C  A  M  A  D  E  S  E  R  T  C
```

1. The _____ Mountains are on Chile's eastern border.
2. Most of Chile's people live in the _____.
3. The _____ _____ is on Chile's western edge.
4. The capital of Chile is _____.
5. _____ are found in the northern part of the Central Valley.
6. There are over 600 _____ within Chile's borders.
7. Earthquakes can cause _____ that travel across the Pacific Ocean.
8. One of the driest places on Earth is the _____ _____.
9. The desert is covered with salt basins and _____ _____.
10. Chile has control of _____ _____, famous for the moai statues.
11. Huge ice fields are found in the _____ region.
12. _____ _____ is the southernmost headland in South America.
13. The _____ were never defeated by the Spanish.
14. The _____ once lived in northern Chile.
15. An _____ is a chain of islands.

SWEDEN

Sweden Quick Facts

Official Name: Kingdom of Sweden
Total area: 450,295 sq km
Population: 9,880,604 (July 2016 est.)
GDP: $498.1 billion (2016 est.)
Government: parliamentary constitutional monarchy
Capital: Stockholm
Motto: For Sweden—With the Times

Sweden is located in the region known as Scandinavia. It shares a border with Norway on the west and Finland on the northeast. The Baltic Sea and the Gulf of Bothnia are located along Sweden's east coast. In the southeast, Sweden borders waters called the Skagerrak, the Kattegat, and the Öresund straits. These waters separate Sweden from Denmark.

The Scandinavian or Kjolen Mountains are located along the western border with Norway. While mountains cover most of Sweden, they are relatively low. The highest point is Kebnekaise at 2,111 m (about 7,000 ft).

Sweden has over 100,000 lakes and many rivers that flow from the mountains through the forested hills and on to the plains and the coast. Sweden's largest lakes are Vänern, Vättern, Mälaren, and Hjälmaren. All Sweden's lakes and more than 24,000 islands are open to the public. Sweden has a tradition of public access to these areas. Sweden was the first country in Europe to create national parks. There are 29 national parks and many other nature reserves and wildlife sanctuaries.

The Swedish economy depends on industries such as iron and steel, precision equipment, wood pulp and paper products, processed foods, and motor vehicles. Agriculture also produces important goods, including barley, wheat, sugar beets, meat, and milk. The fishing industry brings in thousands of tons of fish and seafood from offshore catches, fishing on lakes and rivers, and fish farming.

Fishing Vessel in Grundsund, Sweden

The nation of Sweden was named after the fierce Svea tribe, who eventually became known as the Vikings. Sweden was ruled by an elected king until parliament made the position hereditary in 1544. Now the title of king or queen is passed down through the ruling family. King Carl XVI Gustaf is the head of state. His duties are mostly ceremonial. The head of the government is the prime minister who is elected by the parliament. The Swedish parliament is called the Riksdag.

The Swedes celebrate June 6 as National Day. It commemorates the day in 1523 when Gustav Vasa was crowned king. This led to Sweden becoming an independent state. It also corresponds with the date in 1809 when a new constitution was adopted.

Sweden is sparsely populated. Most of the people live in the south in cities near the coast. Lapland is a province in northern Sweden that has polar and subarctic climates. The nomadic Sami people live in this region. These indigenous people survive by herding reindeer and sheep and by fishing or trapping. Reindeer provide the Sami with transportation, meat, and hides for clothing and shelter.

Sweden is famous for its winter sports. With snow-covered mountains in a majority of the country, downhill skiing, cross-country skiing, and snowboarding are very popular. World Cup downhill skiing events are held in Sweden, and many of the top athletes are Swedish.

World Geography Puzzles: Countries of the World   Sweden

Name: _____ Date: _____

SWEDEN CROSSWORD PUZZLE

Directions: Use the clues below to complete the puzzle about Sweden.

Drum Used by the
Sami People

Across
4. Downhill and cross-country ___ are popular sports in Sweden.
6. Sweden is a ___ with a king or queen as the head of state.
7. The Svea tribe became known as the ___.
9. Sweden was the first European country to create ___ ___.
11. Sweden's largest lake is Lake ___.
13. ___ ___ in Sweden is celebrated on June 6.
14. Sweden is separated from ___ by the Öresund straits.

Down
1. Off Sweden's east coast is the ___ ___ ___.
2. The highest point in Sweden is ___.
3. Sweden's parliament is called the ___.
4. ___ is the region where Sweden is located.
5. The head of government for Sweden is the ___ ___.
8. The Sami herd ___ to survive.
10. The ___ Mountains are located along the western border with Norway.
12. The Sami people are indigenous to the ___ region.

UNITED KINGDOM

United Kingdom Quick Facts

Official Name: United Kingdom of Great Britain and Northern Ireland
Total area: 243,610 sq km
Population: 64,430,428 (July 2016 est.)
GDP: $2.788 trillion (2016 est.)
Government: parliamentary constitutional monarchy
Capital: London
Motto: God and my right

The United Kingdom (UK) is an island nation. It is made up of the island of Great Britain, which includes England, Scotland, and Wales, and Northern Ireland, which is part of the island of Ireland. There are also many smaller islands surrounding Great Britain that are part of the UK. In addition, the United Kingdom is one of 16 realms of the Commonwealth around the world that all share the same monarch as head of state. That monarch is the current queen or king of England.

The head of government in the United Kingdom is the prime minister. The leader of the party in the majority in Parliament usually becomes the prime minister. Parliament is the legislative branch of government. It consists of the House of Lords and the House of Commons. The Supreme Court has 12 justices, including the court president and deputy president.

London is the capital of the United Kingdom and the capital of England. It is located on the River Thames and has long been an important city for trade, shipping, and government. Some of England's best-known landmarks are in London. These include Buckingham Palace, the Tower of London, Westminster Abbey, and Big Ben.

The Houses of Parliament in London

The United Kingdom is surrounded by seas that are extensions of the Atlantic Ocean. The North Sea is off the north and east coasts. The English Channel is between the southern coast of England and the northern coast of France. The Irish Sea separates Great Britain from Ireland on the west. The northwest coast borders the Atlantic Ocean. From the seaports of the UK, explorers, merchants, and the Royal Navy sent ships all over the world to form a vast British Empire. Major port cities include Bristol, Southampton, Portsmouth, Liverpool, London, Belfast, and Aberdeen.

The landscape of the United Kingdom is varied from mountains to low wetlands. Scotland, north-central England, Wales, and Northern Ireland feature mountains. The highest point in the UK is Ben Nevis in Scotland at 1,345 m (4,411 ft). The largest freshwater lake in the UK is Lough Neagh near the center of Northern Ireland. The many lakes in the valleys of the Cumbria Mountains in England have led to the region being called the Lake District. Much of the UK is rolling hills suitable for grazing livestock and producing crops such as grains, oilseeds, potatoes, and other vegetables. In eastern and southern England, there are low-lying areas that flood during heavy rains. Moors are areas of tough grasses and shrubs in both uplands and lowlands. Heather and peat may be harvested from these areas.

Manufacturing once dominated the economy in the United Kingdom. Today, banking, insurance, and business services contribute the most to the economy. In 2016, the citizens of the UK voted to leave the European Union (EU), which is an economic and political union of European nations. Now there is uncertainty about how the UK will deal with other countries over such things as trade agreements and political treaties.

UNITED KINGDOM WORD SCRAMBLE

Directions: Use the clues below to help you unscramble the words associated with the United Kingdom. Write the unscrambled words on the lines provided.

1. AREGT ABINRIT _____
2. OATMLHOMWNEC _____
3. TNAIREAPML _____
4. MESHTA _____
5. ENWSTMSRIET _____
6. NILESGH HENNCAL _____
7. HIRSI AES _____
8. VOLPREILO _____
9. TASCDONL _____
10. GULOH HANGE _____
11. NGNIKAB _____
12. RAUOEEPN _____

1. This island includes England, Scotland, and Wales.
2. The realms of the _____ all share the same monarch as head of state.
3. _____ is the legislative branch of government in the United Kingdom.
4. The River _____ flows through London.
5. _____ Abbey is one of the landmarks found in London.
6. The _____ _____ is found between England and France.
7. The _____ _____ separates Great Britain from Ireland.
8. _____ is one of the major ports of the UK.
9. Ben Nevis in _____ is the highest point in the UK.
10. The largest freshwater lake in the UK is _____ _____ in Northern Ireland.
11. _____ is a major part of the United Kingdom's economy today.
12. Citizens of the UK voted in 2016 to leave the _____ Union.

FRANCE

France Quick Facts

Official Name: French Republic
Total area: 551,500 sq km (met. France)
92,301 sq km (French overseas regions)
Population: 62,814,233 (met. France)
4,021,921 (French overseas regions)
(July 2016 est.)
GDP: $2.737 trillion (2016 est.)
Government: semi-presidential republic
Capital: Paris
Motto: Liberty, Equality, Fraternity

France has historically been a crossroads for the people of Europe. It is located in western Europe, bordering the Atlantic Ocean and the English Channel on the northwest, Spain and Andorra on the southwest, and the Mediterranean Sea on the southeast. On the east, France is bordered by Belgium, Luxembourg, Germany, Switzerland, Italy, and Monaco.

Mainland France, located in Europe, is referred to as metropolitan France. There are five overseas regions that are considered part of France. These are French Guiana, Guadeloupe, Martinique, Mayotte, and Reunion. The people of these regions are French citizens. They can vote for the French president, and they have representatives in the French Parliament. There are also other overseas collectives that are under French administration.

The head of state in France is the president, who is elected by majority vote every five years. The president controls foreign policy and defense. The head of government is the prime minister, who is appointed by the president with the approval of the Parliament. The prime minister is usually from the majority party in the Parliament. The prime minister is in charge of domestic policy and the running of the government. The Parliament is the legislative branch of French government. It consists of the Senate and the National Assembly. The highest courts in France are the Court of Cassation and the Constitutional Council.

France has rebounded from the great devastation suffered during World Wars I and II to become one of the strongest economies in Europe. French exports include wine, cheese, automobiles, electronics, and clothing. Tourism is a major industry in France. It has the third largest income from tourism in the world, with more than 84 million foreign visitors each year. Agricultural products include grains, sugar beets, potatoes, wine grapes, beef, dairy products, and fish.

Vineyards Near Chavignol, France

The rivers of France have long been avenues for the transportation of people and goods throughout France and to the rest of the world. In northern France, the Seine River flows through Paris and empties into the English Channel. The Loire River system drains the central part of France and empties into the Atlantic Ocean near the city of Saint-Nazaire. The Rhone River flows from north to south in the eastern part of France. It empties into the Mediterranean Sea. The Rhine River starts in Switzerland and forms part of France's border with Germany. It flows into the North Sea.

The people of France are some of the most ethnically diverse on Earth. Immigrants from former colonies and possessions in Africa, the Americas, and Asia have settled in France over the last century. More recently, refugees from war-torn areas of the Middle East, Africa, and central and eastern Europe have been allowed into the country. While this creates new pressure on France's resources, it continues the age-old tradition of cultures coming together to produce new trends in art, literature, music, fashion, and food. This has made France a world leader in culture.

World Geography Puzzles: Countries of the World France

Name: _____ Date: _____

FRANCE CODED PUZZLE

Directions: Use the decoder key to fill in the blanks for each statement below.

A	B	C	D	E	F	G	H	I	J	K	L	M	N	O	P	Q	R	S	T	U	V	W	X	Y	Z
1	2	3	4	5	6	7	8	9	10	11	12	13	14	15	16	17	18	19	20	21	22	23	24	25	26

1. The country of France located in Europe is called __ __ __ __ __ __ __ __ __ __ __
   13 5 20 18 15 16 15 12 9 20 1 14
   France.

2. France's southeast coast is on the __ __ __ __ __ __ __ __ __ __ __ __ Sea.
   13 5 4 9 20 5 18 18 1 14 5 1 14

3. The people of France's overseas regions are French __ __ __ __ __ __ __.
   3 9 20 9 26 5 14 19

4. The French head of state is the __ __ __ __ __ __ __ __ __.
   16 18 5 19 9 4 5 14 20

5. The __ __ __ __ __ __ __ __ __ __ __ __ is in charge of domestic policy.
   16 18 9 13 5   13 9 14 9 19 20 5 18

6. The Parliament of France consists of the Senate and the

   __ __ __ __ __ __ __ __ __ __ __ __ __ __.
   14 1 20 9 15 14 1   1 19 19 5 13 2 12 25

7. __ __ __ __ __ __ __ is a major industry in France, with more
   20 15 21 18 9 19 13

   than 84 million foreign visitors each year.

8. The __ __ __ __ __ __ __ __ __ __ flows through Paris.
   19 5 9 14 5   18 9 22 5 18

9. The Rhine River forms part of France's border with __ __ __ __ __ __ __.
   7 5 18 13 1 14 25

10. France is a world leader in __ __ __ __ __ __ __, such as art, literature, music, fashion,
    3 21 12 20 21 18 5

    and food.

11. The population of France is __ __ __ __ __ __ __ __ __ __ diverse.
    5 20 8 14 9 3 1 12 12 25

12. __ __ __ __ __ __ __ __ from war-torn areas of
    18 5 6 21 7 5 5 19

    the world have settled in France.

Bonus: France is known around the world for its

excellent __ __ __ __ __ and __ __ __ __ __ __.
          23 9 14 5   3 8 5 5 19 5

CD-405015 ©Mark Twain Media, Inc., Publishers   16

CROATIA

Croatia Quick Facts

Official Name: Republic of Croatia
Total area: 56,594 sq km
Population: 4,313,707 (July 2016 est.)
GDP: $94.24 billion (2016 est.)
Government: parliamentary republic
Capital: Zagreb
Motto: No official motto

Croatia is a small, crescent-shaped country in southeastern Europe. Its west coast on the Adriatic Sea is called the Dalmatian Coast. Over a thousand islands dot the coastline. Near the coast and along its border with Bosnia and Herzegovina are the low Dinaric Alps. In the part of the country that curves around south of Hungary, there are flat plains with fertile farmland. The Danube River forms the border between Croatia and Serbia. The Drava and Sava Rivers also flow through Croatia and eventually into the Danube River.

The Croat people settled in this area around A.D. 500. Eventually, they became part of the Austro-Hungarian Empire. After World War I, Croats joined with Serbs and Slovenes to form a kingdom called Yugoslavia. After World War II, Yugoslavia became a communist state. This included Bosnia and Herzegovina, Croatia, Macedonia, Slovenia, and Serbia. When the communist system fell in the 1990s, Croatia declared its independence from Yugoslavia in 1991. Croats celebrate June 25 as Statehood Day. This was the date parliament voted for independence. Independence Day is celebrated on October 8 as the date when parliament actually ended constitutional relations with Yugoslavia.

King Tomislav Statue and the Art Pavilion in Zagreb

However, independence did not go smoothly for Croatia. Civil war erupted between the Croats and Serbs. Bitter fighting occurred between 1991 and 1995. Serbia wanted to keep Croatia as part of its republic. Croatia wanted to remain its own nation. Both Serbs and Croats also became involved in the war in Bosnia. Tens of thousands of people were killed. Leaders in both nations were accused of "ethnic cleansing" as they tried to eliminate minority populations within their borders. Muslims were especially targeted during the war. The Serb armies were finally pushed out of Croatia. Most of the people of Serbian descent who had been living in Croatia were also forced out. A peace agreement was signed in December 1995.

Croatia's government has become more stable after the civil war. Croatia joined the North Atlantic Treaty Organization (NATO) in 2009 and the European Union (EU) in 2013. Croatia's head of state is the president, who is elected by popular vote to a five-year term. The prime minister is the head of government. The prime minister is appointed by the president and approved by the parliament. The legislative branch of government is the one-house parliament called the Assembly or Hrvatski Sabor. The Supreme Court is the highest court in the judicial branch.

The economy has been slow since the worldwide economic crisis of 2008. The government has cut spending and raised taxes. Industries include chemicals and plastics, machine tools, electronics, wood products, textiles, and shipbuilding. Many people are employed in service jobs. Tourism is a growing industry in Croatia, mostly in the coastal area. Agricultural products include grains, sugar beets, oilseeds, vegetables, fruits, wine grapes, livestock, and dairy products.

Along the coast, Croatia has a Mediterranean climate. The summers are hot and sunny, and the winters are mild. The northern and eastern parts of the country have a continental climate. The winters are cold, and the summers are warm, with occasional heat waves. The interior gets plentiful rainfall but often feels stifling in the summer because the mountains block the cooling breezes from the sea. The coastal islands are dry, while the mountains receive rain and snow.

World Geography Puzzles: Countries of the World — Croatia

Name: _____ Date: _____

CROATIA LAST LETTER/FIRST LETTER PUZZLE

Directions: Use the clues below to help you fill in the last letter/first letter puzzle. The last letter of one word or phrase will be the first letter of the next word or phrase. The words will go down one column and up the next in a continuous line. Letters have been placed in the puzzle to help you.

1. Alpine mountains found in Croatia
2. Crescent-shaped country in southeastern Europe
3. Sea off the coast of Croatia
4. The people of Croatia are called _____.
5. Croatia fought a bitter war with _____ from 1991 to 1995.
6. The Croats first joined with the _____-_____ Empire.
7. Croatia is a member of the _____ Atlantic Treaty Organization.
8. Croatia shares a border with Bosnia and _____.
9. The Croatian parliament is called the _____.
10. Croatia was once a part of this communist country.
11. _____ in Croatia is conducted mostly on the fertile plains south of Hungary.
12. _____ _____ is a campaign to kill or force out all members of a minority population.
13. The prime minister is the head of _____.
14. Muslims were especially _____ during the war.
15. Croatia's coast is called the _____ Coast.

ITALY

Italy Quick Facts

Official Name: Italian Republic
Total area: 301,340 sq km
Population: 62,007,540 (July 2016 est.)
GDP: $2.221 trillion (2016 est.)
Government: parliamentary republic
Capital: Rome
Motto: Italy is a democratic republic, founded on labor (common saying, not official motto)

Italy is the long, narrow, boot-shaped peninsula that extends from southern Europe into the Mediterranean Sea. Its central position in the Mediterranean has meant that Italy was a crossroads for trade, exploration, and invasion. People from Europe, Africa, the Middle East, and Asia traveled to, from, and through Italy. The Roman Empire, based in Rome, once stretched throughout the known world in ancient times. Merchant ships, explorers, and armies were sent out from Italy's great port cities to the rest of the world. Eventually, Germanic and Asian tribes were able to conquer parts of the Roman Empire and even destroy the city of Rome.

Some of Italy's greatest port cities were Genoa and Pisa on the Ligurian Sea, Naples and Salerno on the Tyrrhenian Sea, and Venice and Ancona on the Adriatic Sea. Each city developed its own powerful navy to defend itself and its merchant ships from pirates and Muslim raiders. After the fall of the Roman Empire, each Italian city-state formed its own government. They often fought each other, as well as foreign invaders.

A Waterfront Street in Venice

The mountains and coastal features of Italy helped to develop the city-states. Cities might be isolated by the mountains or coasts, and they were able to concentrate on ruling their local area. The mountains in northern Italy are part of the Alps. The Italian Alps contain some of the highest peaks in Europe. Gran Paradiso is 4,061 m (13,323 ft) high, Monte Cervino (the Matterhorn) is 4,478 m (14,691 ft) high, and a secondary peak of Mont Blanc located inside Italy is 4,748 m (15,577 ft) high. The Dolomites are part of the Alps in the northeastern part of Italy. The Apennines are the mountains that run down the length of Italy from northwest to southeast and then continue on to the island of Sicily. The Calderone glacier in the Apennines is the southernmost glacier in Europe.

Volcanoes are found on the Flegrei Plain near Naples and on the islands nearby. Mount Vesuvius is a dormant volcano that has had disastrous eruptions in the past. The city of Pompeii was completely buried in ash after an eruption in A.D. 79. Mount Etna is an active volcano located on the island of Sicily. Earthquakes are also common in the central and southern Apennines and on Sicily. These earthquakes kill many people when buildings collapse in populated areas. A village in central Italy was hit with a 6.2 magnitude earthquake in August 2016, and 300 people were killed.

The Italian government became a Fascist dictatorship under Benito Mussolini in the 1920s. He allied Italy with Germany during World War II. After Italy's defeat, the nation became a parliamentary republic with a constitution. Italians celebrate Republic Day on June 2 to commemorate the day in 1946 when they voted to abolish the monarchy and form the Italian Republic. Today, the president is the head of state and the prime minister is the head of government. The president is elected through an electoral college system, and the prime minister is appointed by the president with the approval of the parliament. The parliament consists of a Senate and a Chamber of Deputies. The highest courts in the land are the Supreme Court of Cassation and the Constitutional Court.

World Geography Puzzles: Countries of the World   Italy

Name: _____ Date: _____

ITALY HIDDEN MESSAGE PUZZLE

Directions: Use the clues below to fill in the blanks at the right. When you are finished, unscramble the letters in the circled blanks and write them in the blanks to complete the hidden message at the bottom of the page.

1. A major port city on the Legurian Sea   ___ ___ ___ ___Ⓞ

2. Italy is a boot-shaped ____ surrounded on three sides by water.   ___ ___Ⓞ___ ___ ___ ___ ___

3. Mount ____ is a dormant volcano that destroyed the ancient city of Pompeii.   ___ ___ ___ ___ ___Ⓞ

4. ____ is a major port city on the Adriatic Sea that once had its own powerful navy.   ___ ___ ___ ___ ___ ___

5. ____ is the southernmost glacier in Europe.   ___ ___Ⓞ___ ___ ___ ___

6. Italy was a crossroads for trade, exploration, and ____.   Ⓞ___ ___ ___ ___ ___ ___

7. ____ are common in the central and southern Apennines.   ___ ___ ___ ___ ___ ___Ⓞ___ ___

8. Today, Italy's government is a ____.   Ⓞ___ ___ ___ ___ ___

9. ____ tribes were able to conquer parts of the Roman Empire and destroy the city of Rome.   ___ ___ ___ ___ ___Ⓞ___

10. Monte Cervino, also known as the ____, is one of the tallest peaks in Italy's Alps.   ___ ___ ___ ___ ___ ___ ___ ___ ___

Hidden Message: This large island in the Mediterranean Sea belongs to Italy.

___ ___ ___ ___ ___ ___ ___

RUSSIA

Russia Quick Facts

Official Name: Russian Federation
Total area: 17,098,242 sq km
Population: 142,355,415 (July 2016 est.)
GDP: $3.745 trillion (2016 est.)
Government: semi-presidential federation
Capital: Moscow
Motto: No official motto

Russia is a unique country that spreads across two continents. The Ural Mountains form the dividing line between Europe and Asia. The Caucasus Mountains in the southwest also separate European Russia from the Middle Eastern countries of Asia. About 23% of the land area of Russia is in Europe and 77% is in Asia. However, about 77% of the population lives in European Russia.

Russia is the largest nation in the world in land area. It occupies about one-tenth of all land on Earth. There are a variety of land features and climates throughout the vast Russian nation. The European Plain stretches from the Ural Mountains and Volga River to the western border. The plain is mostly flat with some rolling hills. It is poorly drained in many areas, resulting in marshes. The two largest lakes in Europe, Lake Ladoga and Lake Onega, are located in this region. The continental climate includes hot summers and cold winters. Agriculture is a major industry in this area. Products include grain, sugar beets, sunflower seeds, vegetables, fruits, beef, and dairy products.

The steppes are grassland plains without trees in the central and southern areas of Russia. Today, some areas of the steppes are used for farming.

Areas of coniferous forests, called taiga, extend from the western border of Russia to the Pacific Ocean on the east. While Russia still contains the largest reserve of coniferous forests in the world, much land has been cleared for agriculture. Trees are also cut for lumber and other wood products.

Siberia is the northern part of Russia from the Ural Mountains to the Pacific and Arctic Oceans. This area is known for its frozen tundra, a treeless and marshy plain. There are also rolling hills, plateaus, and mountain ranges. The West Siberian Plain is located between the Ural Mountains and the Yenisey River. It includes large areas of taiga. An oil field with natural gas resources is also found here. This area also includes some of the world's largest swamps.

Major rivers in Russia include the Volga and Dnieper in the west, the Lena and Ob in the center, and the Amur in the east. Lake Baikal in Siberia contains more fresh water than any other lake in the world. Besides the Urals, the mountain ranges of Russia are mostly located along the borders of the country. The Caucasus Mountains contain Russia's and Europe's highest peak, Mt. Elbrus at 5,633 m (18,481 ft). A series of mountain ranges are located along the borders with China and Mongolia. The Kolyma Mountains extend into far northeastern Russia.

Since the fall of communism, Russia has been moving toward a market-based economy. However, most of the wealth and resources are still under the control of the state. Russia is a leading producer of oil, natural gas, steel, and aluminum.

The Russian head of state is the president, who is elected by the people. The head of government is the premier and several deputies and ministers, who are all appointed by the president. The premier must also be approved by the Duma. The legislature is called the Federal Assembly and is composed of the Federation Council and the State Duma. The highest courts are the Supreme Court of the Russian Federation and the Constitutional Court.

The Kremlin, Containing the Central Offices of the Russian Government

RUSSIA CROSSWORD PUZZLE

Directions: Use the clues below to complete the puzzle about Russia.

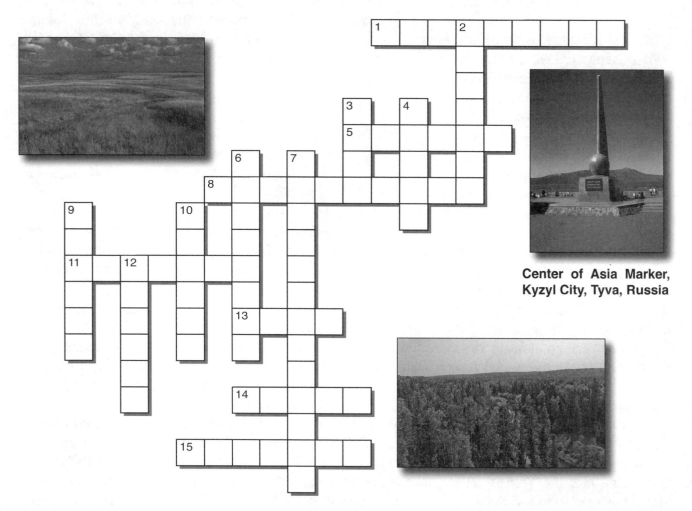

Center of Asia Marker, Kyzyl City, Tyva, Russia

Across
1. The _____ is the head of state in Russia.
5. Some of the world's largest _____ are located in the West Siberian Plain.
8. Russia is a leading producer of _____ _____.
11. _____ is known for its frozen tundra.
13. The _____ Mountains are the dividing line between Europe and Asia.
14. The _____ is a major river in western Russia.
15. The Russian _____ is appointed by the president and approved by the Duma.

Down
2. The _____ are grassland plains without trees.
3. This is the continent where most of Russia's land lies.
4. Areas of coniferous forests are called _____.
6. The _____ Mountains divide southwest Russia from the Middle East.
7. The _____ _____ is mostly flat with some rolling hills, marshes, lakes, and farmland.
9. The capital of Russia is _____.
10. This is the continent where most of Russia's people live.
12. Lake _____ has more fresh water than any other lake in the world.

EGYPT

Egypt Quick Facts

Official Name: Arab Republic of Egypt
Total area: 1,001,450 sq km
Population: 94,666,993 (July 2016 est.)
GDP: $1.105 trillion (2016 est.)
Government: presidential republic
Capital: Cairo
Motto: No official motto

The ancient people in the area that is now Egypt settled there because the Nile River had regular floods that spread fertile soil over the river valleys. They were able to plant crops and raise food, and the Nile provided water for the crops and the people. The area near the Nile River is still the most populated area of Egypt. About 95% of the population lives within 20 km (10 mi.) of the Nile and its delta.

The Nile River Valley in southern Egypt is called Upper Egypt. The Nile flows from south to north to the delta that empties into the Mediterranean Sea. The northern part of Egypt is called Lower Egypt. Cairo, the capital of Egypt, and other major cities, such as Alexandria, Giza, and Tanta, are located in the delta region.

Deserts cover the rest of the country not irrigated by the Nile. From the Nile to the western border is the Western Desert. The Libyan Desert and the Great Sand Sea extend into this area. From the Nile to the Red Sea on the east is the Eastern Desert or Arabian Desert. There are several oases in the Western Desert, such as Siwa, Faiyum, and Farafra. These are areas where vegetation grows around a spring or lake. The water comes from underground rivers or aquifers. Wells are also drilled to bring water to the surface.

Two man-made structures built in the modern age have benefited Egypt and the world. The Suez Canal is a man-made waterway between the Red Sea and the Mediterranean Sea. It was opened November 17, 1869, after more than 15 years of planning and digging. It allows ships to travel from Port Said in the north to Suez in the south or vice versa, instead of having to journey around the continent of Africa. Recent improvements now allow for two-way ship traffic through the canal. The Aswan High Dam was built on the Nile River at Aswan. It was dedicated in January 1971. It backs up the river to create Lake Nassar. The reservoir provides water for people in Egypt and Sudan, and it supports a fishing industry. The dam allows for the control of the flooding of the Nile, and it generates electric power. However, farmland downstream is becoming less fertile because the Nile is no longer allowed to flood and deposit fertile silt on the land. Artificial fertilizers are now needed to keep growing crops.

Egypt is probably best known for the pharaohs who ruled ancient Egypt and built the great pyramids and other monuments. The three largest pyramids were built outside the city of Giza. This includes the Great Pyramid of Khufu or Cheops. The Great Sphinx is also located at this site. Later pharaohs built their tombs and temples near Luxor in what is called the Valley of the Kings. This is where the famous tomb of Tutankhamun is located.

After thousands of years of rule by pharaohs and then long periods under the rule of various empires, such as the Romans and the Ottomans, Egyptians now have a democratic republic. The elected president is the head of state, and the prime minister is the head of government. The prime minister is appointed by the president and approved by the House of Representatives. However, the military is a strong presence and has taken over the government in times of crisis. The legislature is the one-house House of Representatives. The highest courts are the Supreme Constitutional Court, the Court of Cassation, and the Supreme Administrative Court.

World Geography Puzzles: Countries of the World   Egypt

Name: _____ Date: _____

EGYPT WORD SEARCH PUZZLE

Directions: Use the clues below to determine the words associated with Egypt that are in the puzzle. Write the words on the lines provided and find and circle them in the word search puzzle.

```
Q P R E S I D E N T G N E O P F M L S V
N K A W O A S P H N M Q R J B Z F M M T
F B N L U X O R Y X I H H Z G W B M G P
S U E Z C A N A L S D L A S C Y E B R Y
G R C F V J B M K E R D E Z Q D R R E G
O D V Z A E R S Q E P V B R I O L F A E
O V D C N F U R P S T V D T I V I V T R
K V I I V I J K N R C S E V V E R S E
L O X Q V R J O F N P R P Y J W E W A W
T L A K E N A S S A R K N C H E G R N O
A R I M Q N Q A H A H U B Z A A Z T D L
I P X I W U H J N T M C H Z P I P E S K
R Y I J T S Z E R A D Y G H D Y R I E A
D R X Z U U A D H K H B E S G O C O A S
N A P I O N N K O P Q Z M E D H Q Z H S
A M M O X P N S H Z I T R J G Z M M N K
X I T M L A F J I Q Z E Q X F S E H D X
E D T S T Y M M L S P D X C E M Q L Y O
L G Z U D Q N G L P A I O F E D S S R H
A V T P U M U J U N U O C I R T C E L E
```

1. The _____ _____ deposited fertile soil in the river valleys of Egypt.
2. _____ _____ is the southern part of Egypt.
3. The Nile flows through the delta and into the _____ Sea.
4. _____ is a major city in the delta region.
5. _____ is the capital of Egypt.
6. _____ _____ is the northern part of Egypt.
7. The _____ _____ _____ is part of the Western Desert.
8. Faiyum is an _____ where vegetation grows in the desert.
9. The _____ _____ is a man-made waterway between the Red Sea and Mediterranean Sea.
10. The Aswan High Dam created a large reservoir called _____.
11. The dam generates _____ power.
12. The Great _____ of Khufu is located outside Giza.
13. The Valley of the Kings is located near _____.
14. The tomb of _____ is in the Valley of the Kings.
15. Egyptians now have an elected _____ as the head of state.

CD-405015 ©Mark Twain Media, Inc., Publishers   24

NIGERIA

Nigeria Quick Facts

Official Name: Federal Republic of Nigeria
Total area: 923,768 sq km
Population: 186,053,386 (July 2016 est.)
GDP: $1.089 trillion (2016 est.)
Government: federal presidential republic
Capital: Abuja
Motto: Unity and Faith, Peace and Progress

Nigeria is located in West Africa. It borders on the Gulf of Guinea to the south. It has land borders with Benin, Niger, Chad, and Cameroon. The Niger River flows through Nigeria from the west and joins with the Benue River. It then flows south through the middle of the country to the Niger River delta on the coast.

In the north, Nigeria has dry desert plains. The middle and southern parts of Nigeria have plains and highlands covered with tropical grasslands and rain forests. These areas experience dry seasons and rainy seasons. Rainfall in southern Nigeria ranges from 2,000 mm (78.7 in) to over 4,000 mm (157.5 in) a year.

There are hills, mountains, and plateaus in the north-central, southwest, and southeast parts of Nigeria. The highest peak is Chappal Waddi near the border with Cameroon at 2,419 m (7,936 ft). The rare Cross River gorilla is found in the dense mountain forests on the Nigeria-Cameroon border near the beginning of the Cross River. This is a sub-species of the western gorilla. There may be fewer than 250 mature Cross River gorillas in the wild.

While the rain forest areas have diverse plants and animals, the savannas have mostly been cleared of their native animals, such as giraffes, elephants, lions, cheetahs, and antelope. The habitat has been destroyed to make room for agriculture, industry, and people.

Nigeria has the largest petroleum industry in Africa. The oil fields are found in the Niger River delta and offshore. Oil and natural gas are plentiful, yet most of the people still live in poverty. Corruption and a lack of development keep the people from prospering.

Nigeria is the most populated country in Africa. The high growth rate of its population is expected to continue for the near future due to a high birth rate. However, Nigeria has the world's highest number of deaths from HIV/AIDS, estimated at 174,300 in 2014. The people of Nigeria are at high risk for a number of other diseases, such as typhoid fever, malaria, and Ebola virus.

The area around the Niger River was a center for ancient civilizations. The Nok culture lived in central Nigeria more than 2,000 years ago. The Yoruba people have lived on the southwestern plains for thousands of years. Beginning in the 1500s, European slave traders enslaved millions of people from Nigeria and the surrounding countries. Most of these slaves were sent to the Americas. By the early 1900s, the British had defeated the various tribes in Nigeria and set up the colony of Nigeria.

Nigeria gained its independence from the United Kingdom in 1960, and Nigerians celebrate October 1 as Independence Day. The early years of the new nation were marked by corrupt leaders and periods of military rule. In 1999, a new constitution was adopted and a new civilian leader was elected. Elections continue to be marred by interference and violence, but the 2015 election was considered to be well run and fair. The president is both the chief of state and the head of the government. The legislative branch is called the National Assembly. It consists of the Senate and the House of Representatives. The Supreme Court consists of a chief justice and 15 justices.

World Geography Puzzles: Countries of the World   Nigeria

Name: _____   Date: _____

NIGERIA HIDDEN MESSAGE PUZZLE

Directions: Use the clues below to fill in the blanks at the right. When you are finished, unscramble the letters in the circled blanks and write them in the blanks to complete the hidden message at the bottom of the page.

1. Nigeria gets its name from the ____ River.

2. The capital of Nigeria is ____.

3. In the north, Nigeria has dry ____ plains.

4. The ____ grasslands and rain forests have dry seasons and rainy seasons.

5. The Cross River gorilla is found on the border with ____.

6. Nigeria has the largest ____ industry in Africa.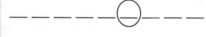

7. Oil and ____ ____ are plentiful.

8. Nigeria is the most ____ country in Africa.

9. European ____ traders took away millions of people from Nigeria and the surrounding area.

10. The legislature of Nigeria is called the National ____.

Hidden Message:

Over 500 __ __ __ __ __ __ __ __ are spoken in Nigeria.

CD-405015 ©Mark Twain Media, Inc., Publishers   26

ZAMBIA

Zambia Quick Facts

Official Name: Republic of Zambia
Total area: 752,618 sq km
Population: 15,510,711 (July 2016 est.)
GDP: $65.17 billion (2016 est.)
Government: presidential republic
Capital: Lusaka
Motto: One Zambia, One Nation

Zambia is a landlocked country in the south-central part of Africa. However, the country has several important rivers and large lakes that provide transportation, water, and power. The Zambezi River flows through its eastern side and along its southern border with Zimbabwe. The Luangwa River in the west and the Kafue River in the country's center also flow into the Zambezi River.

One of the world's great waterfalls is located on the Zambezi River. Victoria Falls is located on the border of Zambia and Zimbabwe, not far from where the borders of Zimbabwe, Botswana, Namibia, and Zambia come to a point. Victoria Falls is 1,708 m (5,604 ft) wide and 108 m (354 ft) high. It is not the widest or highest waterfall in the world, but it claims to be the largest sheet of falling water in the world. Victoria Falls has been named a UNESCO World Heritage Site by the United Nations.

The wide Zambezi River plunges over the falls and then zig-zags through a series of steep canyons. It continues eastward and flows through Lake Kariba on the Zambia-Zimbabwe border and Lago de Cahora Bassa in Mozambique. These lakes have been formed by dams on the river, which provide hydroelectric power for the region. The Zambezi finally flows into the Indian Ocean on the coast of Mozambique.

Victoria Falls

Zambia shares a border with Tanzania on Lake Tanganyika, and Lake Mweru is on the border with the Democratic Republic of the Congo. Lake Bangweulu in the north-central part of Zambia is surrounded by a swamp. Much of the country is flat with small hills. There are savanna grasslands and forests. The climate is tropical with a rainy season from October to April.

There is a great variety of wildlife in Zambia, especially along the Luangwa and Zambezi River valleys. Elephants, giraffes, cheetahs, leopards, lions, hippopotamuses, zebras, crocodiles, hyenas, and warthogs are some of the animals found in Zambia. However, many of these are endangered and are found mostly in the national parks.

After agreements made between the tribal leaders of the area and the British South Africa Company in the 1890s, the area was made a British protectorate. This land was named Northern Rhodesia, after the owner of the company, Cecil Rhodes. The British controlled the colony from 1924 to 1964. The country chose the name Zambia when it gained its independence in 1964.

The British found valuable mineral resources in Zambia. Copper continues to be its number-one export. Cobalt, zinc, lead, coal, emeralds, gold, silver, and uranium are some of Zambia's other resources. Agricultural products include corn, sorghum, rice, sunflower seeds, vegetables, sugarcane, and coffee.

Despite complaints of fraud and violence, Zambia's government is democratically elected. The president, who is elected by majority vote, is the chief of state and head of government. The legislative branch is the National Assembly. The highest courts in the land are the Supreme Court and the Constitutional Court.

World Geography Puzzles: Countries of the World Zambia

Name: _____ Date: _____

ZAMBIA WORD SCRAMBLE

Directions: Use the clues below to help you unscramble the words associated with Zambia. Write the unscrambled words on the lines provided.

1. RKBAIA
   _____

2. ADOIHSRE
   _____

3. MABIWEZB
   _____

4. ICRTOAVI   LLSFA
   _____

5. NWBLUGEUA
   _____

6. CREPOP
   _____

7. LSERDAOP
   _____

8. UALGNAW
   _____

9. NKATIAAGNY
   _____

10. YRLCEDCIHTROE
    _____

11. EMUWR
    _____

12. MNERTOENGV
    _____

1. Lake formed by damming the Zambezi River

2. Zambia was once called Northern _____.

3. The Zambezi River is the border between Zambia and _____.

4. Unesco World Heritage Site found on the Zambezi River

5. Lake surrounded by swamp

6. Major mineral resource exported by Zambia

7. One of the animals found in Zambia

8. River in the west where a great many wild animals are found

9. Lake on the border between Zambia and Tanzania

10. Dams on the Zambezi provide _____ power.

11. Lake on the border between Zambia and the Democratic Republic of the Congo

12. The president is the head of state and the head of _____.

SOUTH AFRICA

South Africa Quick Facts

Official Name: Republic of South Africa
Total area: 1,219,090 sq km
Population: 54,300,704 (July 2016 est.)
GDP: $736.3 billion (2016 est.)
Government: parliamentary republic
Capital: Cape Town (legislative), Pretoria (administrative), Bloemfontein (judicial)
Motto: Diverse people unite

South Africa is the large country at the extreme southern end of Africa. When European explorers and traders began sailing around Africa to get to Asia, they began stopping in South Africa to take on supplies. The Dutch established Cape Town in 1652, and soon Dutch Afrikaners settled in the area.

When the British took over the Cape Town colony in 1806, the Dutch, called Boers or "farmers" by the British, moved north. They took territory from the native Africans to establish their farms and settlements. The discovery of diamonds, gold, and other mineral resources made this a valuable colony for European nations. After two wars between the British and Afrikaners (Boers), the Union of South Africa was created in 1910 as a part of the British Empire, with British and Afrikaners ruling together.

The native Africans, who were the majority of the population, had no role in the government. In 1948, the government began the policy called apartheid, which was a separation of the races. The black majority received very little of the government resources for education, health care, and housing. Opposition protesters in the African National Congress, such as Nelson Mandela, were sent to prison for decades.

After uprisings by black citizens in South Africa and international boycotts by Western countries, institutions, and businesses, South Africa began to change its government so that the majority could rule. The first multi-racial elections were held in 1994. Nelson Mandela was elected president. He had been released from prison in 1990 after 27 years.

The president of South Africa is both the head of state and head of government. The president is not elected directly by the people. The president is elected by the National Assembly. The National Assembly, which is elected by the people, is one house of the Parliament. The other house is the National Council of Provinces. The highest courts are the Supreme Court of Appeals and the Constitutional Court.

South Africa is a land of high plateaus. The grasslands are called highveld, and the plains dotted with trees are called bushveld. Along the outer rim of the country in the south and east are mountainous areas called the Great Escarpment. The Drakensberg Mountains in the east are high jagged peaks. The highest peak is Njesuthi at 3,408 m (11,181 ft). The Blyde River Canyon is also in the Drakensbergs. It is one of the world's largest canyons at 26 km (16 mi.) long and 762 m (2,500 ft) deep. Table Mountain is a flat-topped mountain that is a well-known landmark overlooking the city of Cape Town.

Devil's Peak and Table Mountain Near Cape Town

The Kalahari Desert is located in the north and central part of South Africa. While the Orange and Vaal Rivers flow through the middle of the country, much of the nation suffers from a shortage of water. Dams and reservoirs along the river have been developed to help provide water for irrigation and drinking water for the population.

South Africa has a major health problem with the HIV/AIDS epidemic. An estimated 7 million people were living with HIV/AIDS in 2015. That is the world's highest HIV/AIDS population. It is estimated that 182,400 people died from this disease in 2015. The government is working to combat the epidemic with education and treatment programs.

South Africa Coded Puzzle

Directions: Use the decoder key to fill in the blanks for each statement below.

A	B	C	D	E	F	G	H	I	J	K	L	M	N	O	P	Q	R	S	T	U	V	W	X	Y	Z
3	6	9	12	14	17	20	23	26	24	21	18	15	1	4	7	10	13	16	19	22	25	11	8	5	2

1. The Dutch who settled in South Africa were called __ __ __ __ __ __ __ __ __.
   3 17 13 26 21 3 1 14 13 16

2. The Dutch established __ __ __ __ __ __ __ __ in 1652.
   9 3 7 14 19 4 11 1

3. The __ __ __ __ __ __ __ and the Boers fought for control of South Africa.
   6 13 26 19 26 16 23

4. European nations wanted to control the region because it contained

   __ __ __ __ __ __ __ __, gold, and other mineral resources.
   12 26 3 15 4 1 12 16

5. Native Africans were the __ __ __ __ __ __ __ __, but they had no role in the government.
   15 3 24 4 13 26 19 5

6. __ __ __ __ __ __ __ __ __ was the South African policy to keep the races separate.
   3 7 3 13 19 23 14 26 12

7. __ __ __ __ __ __ __ __ __ __ __ __ was a black South African protester who was
   1 14 18 16 4 1 15 3 1 12 14 18 3

   imprisoned for 27 years and who then became the president.

8. The high jagged mountains in South Africa are called the

   __ __ __ __ __ __ __ __ __ __ __ Mountains.
   12 13 3 21 14 1 16 6 14 13 20

9. The grasslands on the plateau are called __ __ __ __ __ __ __ __.
   23 26 20 23 25 14 18 12

10. The __ __ __ __ __ __ __ __ Desert is in north and central South Africa.
    21 3 18 3 23 3 13 26

11. Dams and __ __ __ __ __ __ __ __ __ __ on the Orange and Vaal Rivers provide water
    13 14 16 14 13 25 4 26 13 16

    for irrigation and people.

12. South Africa has the world's largest __ __ __ __ __ __ __ __ __ __ living with HIV/AIDS.
    7 4 7 22 18 3 19 26 4 1

Bonus: The land north of the Vaal River in South Africa is known as the

__ __ __ __ __ __ __ __ __.
19 13 3 1 16 25 3 3 18

IRAQ

Iraq Quick Facts

Official Name: Islamic Republic of Iraq
Total area: 438,317 sq km
Population: 38,146,025 (July 2016 est.)
GDP: $596.7 billion (2016 est.)
Government: federal parliamentary republic
Capital: Baghdad
Motto: Independence, freedom, the Islamic Republic

Iraq is located in the Middle East. Since ancient times, the area was called Mesopotamia, meaning "the land between the rivers." The Tigris is the northern river, and the Euphrates is the southern river in Iraq. Both rivers begin in the mountains of Turkey, flow through Syria, and then across Iraq. They join just north of Basra and then empty into the Persian Gulf.

Some of the world's earliest civilizations, such as the Sumerians and the Assyrians, settled in this area because of the fertile land fed by the rivers. Today, there are dams built on the rivers to control the flooding and irrigation. However, when the government began water control measures, this led to water shortages in areas that used to be marshlands. Agriculture is still important in Iraq, with irrigated farmland along the rivers, marshland in the south, and pasture land in the northeast. Date palm trees are grown near the rivers. Other crops include wheat, fruit, and vegetables. Livestock raised include sheep and water buffalo.

The climate in much of Iraq is arid and desert-like. The Syrian Desert covers much of the southwestern part of Iraq. Summers are hot and dry while winters are cooler, but temperatures rarely reach below freezing. Most of the average annual rainfall of 102–178 mm (4–7 in) falls from November through April.

Tigris River Flowing Through Baghdad

There are several large lakes in Iraq that hold water for use year-round. Lake Tharthar is located in northern Iraq between the Tigris and Euphrates Rivers. It has been enlarged to catch the floodwaters of the Tigris and now is a freshwater reservoir that is 97 km (60 mi.) long. Other lakes include Habbaniyah Lake and Razazah Lake.

Iraq has become important to western nations in modern times because of its vast reserves of petroleum. Iraq has the second-largest proven oil reserves in the world, behind Saudi Arabia. Iraq also has large natural gas reserves. It is a member of the Organization of Petroleum Exporting Countries (OPEC). While international sanctions and wars have decreased the output of petroleum from Iraq during recent years, petroleum accounts for about 95% of all Iraqi exports.

After World War I, Iraq was made a protectorate of the United Kingdom. In 1932, it gained independence and became a kingdom. In 1958, a republic was established, but Iraq was ruled by a series of military strongmen. Saddam Hussein was the last such leader. During two Persian Gulf Wars in 1991 and 2003–2011, United Nations coalition forces led by the United States invaded Iraq. Saddam Hussein was removed from power, and the Iraqi people gained control of the government.

The Iraqis approved a new constitution in 2005, and they elected a Council of Representatives. This is the legislative branch of the government. The president is the chief of state, who is elected by the Council of Representatives. The prime minister is the head of government, who is nominated by the president and approved by the Council. The highest courts are the Federal Supreme Court and the Court of Cassation.

War against the Islamic State of Iraq and Syria (ISIS) continues as Iraqi troops try to recapture territory in the western and northern part of Iraq. This Islamic extremist terrorist group wants to set up its own nation in Iraq, Syria, and other parts of the Middle East.

Iraq Crossword Puzzle

Directions: Use the clues below to complete the puzzle about Iraq.

Across
4. Areas that used to be ____ are drying up due to water control measures.
7. Iraq has vast reserves of ____.
10. Major northern river in Iraq
12. ____ ____ trees are grown near the rivers in Iraq.
13. After World War I, Iraq was a protectorate of the ____ ____.
15. Early civilization that developed where Iraq is now

Down
1. ____ ____ was the last military strongman to rule Iraq.
2. Major southern river in Iraq
3. ____ ____ is a large freshwater reservoir.
5. The United States invaded Iraq during two ____ ____ ____.
6. The Iraqi people elected a Council of ____.
8. Name that means "the land between the rivers"
9. Capital of Iraq
11. Only ____ ____ has more oil than Iraq.
14. Iraq went from a ____ to a republic in 1958.

INDIA

India Quick Facts

Official Name: Republic of India
Total area: 3,287,263 sq km
Population: 1,266,883,598 (July 2016 est.)
GDP: $8.721 trillion (2016 est.)
Government: federal parliamentary republic
Capital: New Delhi
Motto: Truth alone triumphs

The nation of India is located on a large peninsula that juts into the Indian Ocean in the southern part of Asia. The Arabian Sea is on the west, and the Bay of Bengal is on the east. This peninsula is called the Indian Subcontinent. It is on the Indian Plate, which is a tectonic plate that moved north and collided with the Eurasian Plate over millions of years.

The Himalaya Mountains were formed in the area where the tectonic plates collided. These are the highest mountains in the world. The highest peak in India is Kangchenjunga at 8,598 m (28,209 ft). It is located on the border with Nepal.

South of the Himalayas is the fertile Indo-Gangetic Plain, also called the Great Plain or the North Indian Plain. It covers most of northern India. The silt on the plain was deposited by rivers running out of the Himalayas. The Ganges River begins in the Himalayas and then flows eastward across the plain where it is joined by many tributary rivers. The Brahmaputra River, in the neighboring country of Bangladesh, joins the Ganges, and the combined rivers then flow into the Bay of Bengal. The Indus River begins in the Tibetan Himalayas, flows through the northwestern tip of India, and then southwest through Pakistan to the Arabian Sea. South of the plains are plateaus, and near the southern coasts are lower mountains called the Western Ghats and the Eastern Ghats.

Agriculture is a major industry in India. Almost half the workforce is involved in agriculture. Products raised include rice, wheat, cotton, jute, and tea. However, services are the major source of economic growth. India is a major exporter of information technology services, business outsourcing services, and software workers. India is also a major exporter of petroleum products, textiles, chemicals, and pharmaceuticals.

India has the second-largest population in the world. Large cities, such as New Delhi, Mumbai, Kolkata, and Bangalore, contain vast slum areas. The rural areas also contain a large number of people living in poverty. In 2015, an estimated 12.4% of the population lived below the official poverty level of $1.90 per day. This is actually an improvement in recent years as electricity has been extended to rural villages. Electricity has freed up more time for women to work outside the home and for girls to get an education.

Mumbai Train Station

India got its name from the Indus River. From the Indus Valley civilization, to the Aryans, who spoke Sanskrit, to the Gupta Empire, the Muslim Delhi Sultanate, and the Mughal Dynasty, India has been a part of many different dynasties and empires. After the Europeans arrived in India, trading bases were established. Eventually, the British Empire gained control of most of the country in 1757. Violent uprisings by the Indian people were put down by the British. Finally, after years of nonviolent protests led by Mohandas Gandhi and Jawaharial Nehru, India was granted independence in 1947. For most of its history, the areas now known as Pakistan and Bangladesh were part of the nation of India. Pakistan was separated from India as an independent nation in 1947. Bangladesh, which had been part of Pakistan, became independent in 1971.

India Word Scramble

Directions: Use the clues below to help you unscramble the words associated with India. Write the unscrambled words on the lines provided.

1. BUNTNSTNEICO   1. The Indian _____ is on the Indian Plate, which collided with the Eurasian Plate.

2. YALHAIMA   2. The _____ Mountains are the highest in the world.

3. EANNHGKJUNAGC   3. _____ is the highest peak in India.

4. IOND - CNETGIAG   4. The _____-_____ Plain covers most of northern India.

5. AHUMTARBARP   5. The _____ River joins the Ganges in Bangladesh.

6. LBAGEN   6. The Ganges River flows into the Bay of _____.

7. ABIAARN   7. The Indus River flows into the _____ Sea.

8. WREESTN THSGA   8. Low mountains near the west coast of India are called the _____ _____.

9. CURGAUELITR   9. Almost half of the workforce is involved in _____.

10. TOONYCEHGL   10. Many workers provide information _____ services.

11. KANTPIAS   11. _____ and Bangladesh used to be part of India.

12. VPTROYE   12. In city slums and rural villages, many Indian people live in _____.

CHINA

China Quick Facts

Official Name: People's Republic of China
Total area: 9,596,960 sq km
Population: 1,373,541,278 (July 2016 est.)
GDP: $21.27 trillion (2016 est.)
Government: communist state
Capital: Beijing
Motto: No official motto

For thousands of years, China has had a thriving civilization. The inventive Chinese were the first to develop paper, printing, gunpowder, silk, the magnetic compass, and many other products and processes. A series of leaders founded dynasties that ruled China, starting in 2070 B.C. The country was first united under an emperor in 221 B.C. This was called the Qin or Ch'in Dynasty. The Qing Dynasty was the last imperial dynasty in China. A revolution resulted in a republic being established in 1912. After a civil war between communists and Chinese nationalists, the communists took over the government in 1949. The nationalists fled to the island of Taiwan and set up the Republic of China. However, the government in mainland China does not recognize the Republic of China. They claim Taiwan as one of the provinces of the People's Republic of China. Since 1971, the United Nations has recognized only the People's Republic of China.

Today the head of state is the president, who is indirectly elected by the National People's Congress. The head of government is the premier, who is nominated by the president and approved by the Congress. The National People's Congress is the legislative branch of the Chinese government. The members are indirectly elected by regional, provincial, and municipal people's congresses and by the army. Only members of the Chinese Communist Party and other approved candidates can be elected. The highest court is the Supreme People's Court.

China has a wide variety of geographic features. The west has mountain ranges, plateaus, and deserts. In the east, there are hills, plains, and river deltas. The climate ranges from tropical in the south to subarctic in the north. The Himalaya Mountains along China's border with Nepal are the highest mountains in the world. China's, and the world's, highest peak is Mt. Everest at 8,850 m (29,025 ft.). The Taklamakan Desert is the largest desert in China. It is called the "sea of death." The Gobi Desert begins east of the Taklamakan and continues along the border with Mongolia.

The rivers in China have been important for agriculture, transportation, and in modern times, the generation of hydroelectric power. The Yangtze River is the third longest river in the world. It flows from west to east across the country and empties into the East China Sea near Shanghai. The Three Gorges Dam on the Yangtze River is the world's largest hydroelectric dam. In addition to generating electricity, it is designed to control flooding downstream and improve shipping on the river. However, the reservoir created by the dam is 660 km (410 mi.) long.

Qutang Gorge on the Yangtze River

This displaced 1.24 million people, covered important archaeological sites, and has changed the environment in the area greatly. The Yellow River, or Huang He River, flows into the Bohai Sea. It is considered the "cradle of Chinese civilization" since this was where people first settled, built small villages, grew crops, and began the Chinese culture.

The wildlife in China is varied. Snow leopards, river dolphins, and giant pandas are some of the rarest animals found in China. While increasing development for agriculture, industry, and the growing population continues to destroy wildlife habitat, China has set aside more than 2,500 nature reserves.

World Geography Puzzles: Countries of the World

China

Name: _____ Date: _____

CHINA WORD SEARCH PUZZLE

Directions: Use the clues below to determine the words associated with China that are in the puzzle. Write the words on the lines provided and find and circle them in the word search puzzle.

```
V I R G O F B G B P N O I T U L O V E R
N C S R E M X R O V C Z G M Z H E L I V
M Q A T O D T Y V F G O E Y R I A U B A
O Q D L S J O G A C E S M H R C I O F T
N M J Y S I Y U I B V P Q P I T O X A B
G W A X N E M E C E P P G A D A K K X
O R K L L A H U B D S F O W H S L H K O
L R V L W U S O M P G L W C Z A S B A P
I O O Q T G B T C M O T R N M E X E A E
A W J P R J P I Y E O O L A A I B Q L L
V N Y W B R L G A U Y C K D E X X X B K
I P G I C B A H F A S A S S E R G N O C
S P F U U R C V S Z N T A L U U I M U A
N X P P S R O A T C Y Y E S K E A W W G
I Z E G A S Y O D O A N Q W Z C A X Q N
H R W J Z M C I O L F F M T E V A V O I
P X P O S O U X A Y F R G C K M K V M J
L N J P C C R M Y P T N W W Y P R T H I
O Z B Z W V I Z D G A T A I W A N U I E
D U B M L H R O M Y S N O X F Q L E O B
```

1. The Chinese were the first to invent the magnetic _____.
2. The Qin _____ was the first to be led by an emperor.
3. A _____ brought an end to the last imperial dynasty in China.
4. China became a _____ in 1912.
5. The _____ took over China's government in 1949.
6. Chinese nationalists set up their own government on the island of _____.
7. The capital of the People's Republic of China is _____.
8. The legislature is the National People's _____.
9. The highest mountains in the world are the _____ Mountains.
10. The _____ Desert is called the "sea of death."
11. The Gobi Desert is along China's border with _____.
12. The Three Gorges Dam is on the _____ River.
13. The _____ River is called the "cradle of Chinese civilization."
14. The reservoir created by the Three Gorges Dam covered up important _____ sites.
15. River _____ are some of the rarest animals found in China.

CD-405015 ©Mark Twain Media, Inc., Publishers   36

JAPAN

Japan Quick Facts

Official Name: Japan
Total area: 377,915 sq km
Population: 126,702,133 (July 2016 est.)
GDP: $4.932 trillion (2016 est.)
Government: parliamentary constitutional monarchy
Capital: Tokyo
Motto: No official motto

Japan has four main islands and nearly 4,000 smaller ones. The main islands from north to south are Hokkaido, Honshu, Shikoku, and Kyushu. Many of Japan's largest cities, such as Tokyo, Yokohama, Osaka, and Kyoto, are located on the largest island, Honshu.

Most of Japan's cities are located on or near the coast. The interiors of the islands are covered with mountains and forests. The mountains that run down the middle of Honshu are called the Japanese Alps. Many of Japan's mountains are active or dormant volcanoes. Mt. Fuji, which is the highest peak at 3,776 m (12,388 ft), is an active volcano.

Mt. Fuji

Just off the Pacific Coast of Japan is an area where three of Earth's tectonic plates meet. This area is seismically active. There are an average of 1,500 earthquakes a year in Japan. Most of these are only tremors, but there are major earthquakes occasionally. The earthquakes can also cause tsunamis, which are large sea waves that smash into the shore and can travel great distances inland. In fact, *tsunami* is a Japanese word that means "harbor wave." Tsunamis are caused by earthquakes, volcanic eruptions, or landslides that occur under the water or along a coast.

In March 2011, a 9.0-magnitude earthquake occurred off the northeastern coast of Japan. The tsunami that followed killed nearly 16,000 people, with about 2,500 still listed as missing. It destroyed hundreds of thousands of homes and businesses, wrecked roads and shipping ports, and caused the meltdown of nuclear reactors at the Fukushima-Daiichi Nuclear Power Plant. The earthquake actually moved the island of Honshu 2.4 m (8 ft) eastward.

In the north, Japan's island of Hokkaido is only 40 km (26 mi.) from the Russian island of Sakhalin. At one time, Japan occupied the island, and there is still no treaty agreeing to the Russian takeover of the island after World War II. In the south, the Korea Strait is the body of water that separates Japan from South Korea. There are about 200 km (120 mi.) between the two countries. The far southern Ryukyu Islands stretch almost to Taiwan.

The climate in Japan ranges from subarctic in the north to subtropical in the south. Central and northern Japan have areas noted for winter sports. Spring in the Tokyo area is famous for the cherry blossoms. There is a rainy season from May to July, depending on the latitude. Typhoons (Pacific hurricanes) may occur from July to October.

While most of the land is mountainous, there are farming areas. Rice is a major crop, along with vegetables, fruits, tea, flowers, and livestock. Seafood is a main source of nutrition. Except for rice, the Japanese have to import a great deal of their food. Raw materials and fossil fuels for industry are also imported. Since World War II, the Japanese economy has thrived on manufacturing. It is one of the world's greatest producers of motor vehicles, electronics, and ships.

The head of state is the hereditary emperor of Japan. This is mostly a ceremonial position. The head of government is the prime minister who is the leader of the majority party in the House of Representatives. The legislature is the Diet, which consists of the elected House of Councillors and the House of Representatives. The Supreme Court is the highest court in Japan.

World Geography Puzzles: Countries of the World   Japan

Name: _____ Date: _____

Japan Hidden Message Puzzle

Directions: Use the clues below to fill in the blanks at the right. When you are finished, unscramble the letters in the circled blanks and write them in the blanks to complete the hidden message at the bottom of the page.

1. Mountains down the middle of Honshu   _Ⓞ_ _ _ _ _ _ Ⓞ_ _ _

2. Japan has nearly 4,000 small _____.   Ⓞ_ _ _ _ _ _

3. The northernmost big island   _ _ _ _ _ _Ⓞ_

4. Japan's capital   _Ⓞ_ _ _

5. Japan is near an area where three _____ plates meet.   _ _ _ _ _ _ _Ⓞ

6. Many of Japan's mountains are _____.   Ⓞ_ _ _ _ _ _ _ _

7. A _____ smashes into shore and can travel great distances inland.   _ _ _ _ _ _Ⓞ

8. Typhoons, or Pacific _____, may occur from July to October.   _ _ _Ⓞ_ _ _ _ _

9. The _____ of Japan is the hereditary head of state.   _ _ _Ⓞ_ _ _

10. The prime minister is the leader of the _____ party in the House of Representatives.   _ _ _ _ _ _Ⓞ_

Hidden Message: _ _ _ _ _ _ _ _ _ _ water was released from the nuclear reactors damaged by the 2011 earthquake and tsunami.

AUSTRALIA

Australia Quick Facts

Official Name: Commonwealth of Australia
Total area: 7,741,220 sq km
Population: 22,992,654 (July 2016 est.)
GDP: $1.189 trillion (2016 est.)
Government: parliamentary democracy under a constitutional monarchy
Capital: Canberra
Motto: No official motto

Australia has many species of plants and animals that are not found anywhere else on Earth. Because the continent of Australia is surrounded by water, animals were not able to migrate in or out, so they developed in unique ways. The kangaroo, platypus, koala, and echidna are just a few of the animals that are only found in the wild in Australia.

The environment has shaped how plants and animals have adapted and survived. Nearly one-third of the country is desert. The Great Sandy Desert, Gibson Desert, and the Great Victoria Desert cover the western and central part of Australia. The Great Dividing Range of mountains runs along the eastern rim of the country. From there, water either flows to the east toward the coast or to the west into the Great Artesian Basin. This is the largest source of groundwater in the world. There are also areas of rain forest along the eastern coast, especially in the northeast, southeast, and on the island of Tasmania. The Great Barrier Reef is a 2,300-km (1,400 mi.) system of coral reefs off the northeast coast.

Australia's largest river system is the Murray-Darling system. The Murray River forms most of the border between New South Wales and Victoria. The Darling River flows toward the southwest from the mountains and across New South Wales before joining with the Murray. Two other large tributaries of the Murray River are the Lachlan River and the Murrumbidgee River. The Murray River flows into the Indian Ocean at Encounter Bay near Goolwa, South Australia. Another group of rivers flows into Lake Eyre in South Australia. Cooper Creek and the Diamantina River provide water for this largest salt water lake in

Confluence of the Murray and Darling Rivers

Australia. However, most of the time, Lake Eyre is a dry salt flat. It only receives water when excess monsoon rains fall in Queensland and the Northern Territory. Other major rivers include the Gascoyne River in Western Australia and Victoria River in the Northern Territory.

The first people to settle in Australia migrated from Southeast Asia more than 40,000 years ago over land bridges that once existed when the ocean levels were lower. Because they had little contact with other people, they developed a unique culture. The Aborigines, as they were called by Europeans, were hunter-gatherers. They developed weapons, such as spears, clubs, and boomerangs, and they trained dingoes, the wild dogs of Australia, to help them hunt. There were more than 500 different tribes at one time.

Dutch explorers first sailed to Australia in 1606. In 1770, Captain James Cook claimed the east coast for Great Britain. By 1829, Great Britain had claimed the entire continent. The first British colony in Australia was established in the area of Sydney Harbor in January 1788. Many of the first British settlers were convicts who were sent to New South Wales as punishment. At first, the British and the Aborigines were friendly to each other as they traded goods and food. However, when the British started coming in greater numbers, the Aborigines were pushed off their land. Some Aborigines fought back, and they proved to be fierce warriors. Warfare, disease, and malnutrition reduced the population of Aborigines to about 40,000 by 1965. Only in recent years has the government started working to protect Aborigines and restore their rights.

Australia Last Letter/First Letter Puzzle

Directions: Use the clues below to help you fill in the last letter/first letter puzzle. The last letter of one word will be the first letter of the next word. The words will go down one column and up the next in a continuous line. Letters have been placed in the puzzle to help you.

1. A tributary of the Murray River
2. Lake that is usually a dry salt flat
3. _____ called the natives they found in Australia Aborigines.
4. The first British settlement was in the area of _____ _____.
5. The Murray-Darling is the largest _____ _____ in Australia.
6. Warfare, disease, and _____ reduced the numbers of Aborigines.
7. _____ _____ _____ began as a colony for British convicts.
8. The Murray River enters the Indian Ocean near Goolwa, _____ _____.
9. The Great _____ Basin is the largest source of groundwater in the world.
10. There are areas of rain forest in the _____.
11. At first, the British and Aborigines got along as they _____ with each other.
12. The mountains of the Great _____ Range run along the eastern rim of the country.
13. The _____ _____ Desert is in the south central part of Australia.
14. The continent of _____ is surrounded by water so many unique plants and animals are found there.
15. The _____ were hunter-gatherers who trained dingoes to help them hunt.

Answer Keys

Canada Crossword Puzzle (p. 2)

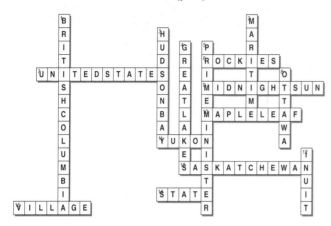

Chile Word Search Puzzle (p. 10)

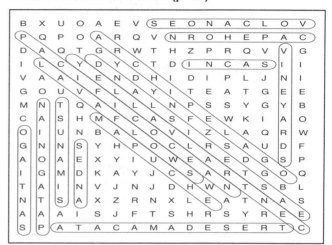

Mexico Hidden Message Puzzle (p. 4)
1. SPAIN
2. RIO GRANDE
3. REPUBLIC
4. ORIENTAL
5. OCCIDENTAL
6. SEA LEVEL
7. ACAPULCO
8. PLATEAU
9. OFFSHORE
10. CANYON

Hidden Message: VOLCANOES

Panama Last Letter/First Letter Puzzle (p. 6)
1. ISTHMUS
2. SOUTH
3. HYDROELECTRIC
4. COLOMBIA
5. ARMY
6. YELLOW FEVER
7. RIO CHAGRES
8. SHIP
9. PANAMA
10. ANCIENT
11. TRANSFERRING
12. GATUN
13. NAVIGATE
14. EFFORT
15. TWENTIETH

Brazil Coded Puzzle (p. 8)
1. BRASILIA
2. PORTUGAL
3. LEGISLATURE
4. RAIN FOREST
5. AMAZON
6. PANTANAL
7. HIGHLANDS
8. VENEZUELA
9. SOYBEANS
10. URANIUM

Bonus: CHILE and ECUADOR

1. ANDES
2. CENTRAL VALLEY
3. PACIFIC OCEAN
4. SANTIAGO
5. VINEYARDS
6. VOLCANOES
7. TSUNAMIS
8. ATACAMA DESERT
9. LAVA FLOWS
10. EASTER ISLAND
11. PATAGONIAN
12. CAPE HORN
13. MAPUCHE
14. INCAS
15. ARCHIPELAGO

Sweden Crossword Puzzle (p. 12)

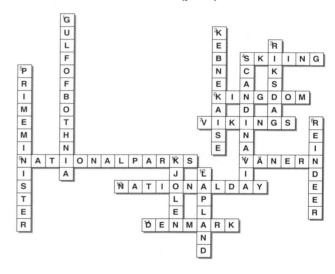

United Kingdom Word Scramble (p. 14)
1. GREAT BRITAIN
2. COMMONWEALTH
3. PARLIAMENT
4. THAMES
5. WESTMINSTER
6. ENGLISH CHANNEL
7. IRISH SEA
8. LIVERPOOL
9. SCOTLAND
10. LOUGH NEAGH
11. BANKING
12. EUROPEAN

France Coded Puzzle (p. 16)
1. METROPOLITAN
2. MEDITERRANEAN
3. CITIZENS
4. PRESIDENT
5. PRIME MINISTER
6. NATIONAL ASSEMBLY
7. TOURISM
8. SEINE RIVER
9. GERMANY
10. CULTURE
11. ETHNICALLY
12. REFUGEES

Bonus: WINE and CHEESE

Croatia Last Letter/First Letter Puzzle (p. 18)
1. DINARIC
2. CROATIA
3. ADRIATIC
4. CROATS
5. SERBIA
6. AUSTRO-HUNGARIAN
7. NORTH
8. HERZEGOVINA
9. ASSEMBLY
10. YUGOSLAVIA
11. AGRICULTURE
12. ETHNIC CLEANSING
13. GOVERNMENT
14. TARGETED
15. DALMATIAN

Italy Hidden Message Puzzle (p. 20)
1. GENOA
2. PENINSULA
3. VESUVIUS
4. VENICE (or ANCONA)
5. CALDERONE
6. INVASION
7. EARTHQUAKES
8. REPUBLIC
9. GERMANIC
10. MATTERHORN

Hidden Message: SARDINIA

Russia Crossword Puzzle (p. 22)

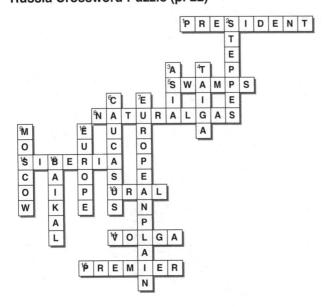

Egypt Word Search Puzzle (p. 24)

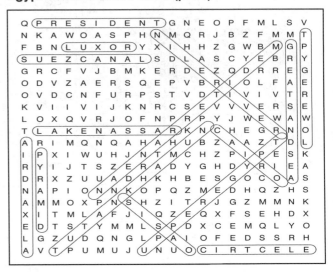

1. NILE RIVER
2. UPPER EGYPT
3. MEDITERRANEAN
4. ALEXANDRIA
5. CAIRO
6. LOWER EGYPT
7. GREAT SAND SEA
8. OASIS
9. SUEZ CANAL
10. LAKE NASSAR
11. ELECTRIC
12. PYRAMID
13. LUXOR
14. TUTANKHAMUN
15. PRESIDENT

Nigeria Hidden Message Puzzle (p. 26)
1. NIGER
2. ABUJA
3. DESERT
4. TROPICAL
5. CAMEROON
6. PETROLEUM
7. NATURAL GAS
8. POPULATED
9. SLAVE
10. ASSEMBLY

Hidden Message: LANGUAGES

Zambia Word Scramble (p. 28)
1. KARIBA
2. RHODESIA
3. ZIMBABWE
4. VICTORIA FALLS
5. BANGWEULU
6. COPPER
7. LEOPARDS
8. LUANGWA
9. TANGANYIKA
10. HYDROELECTRIC
11. MWERU
12. GOVERNMENT

South Africa Coded Puzzle (p. 30)
1. AFRIKANERS
2. CAPE TOWN
3. BRITISH
4. DIAMONDS
5. MAJORITY
6. APARTHEID
7. NELSON MANDELA
8. DRAKENSBERG
9. HIGHVELD
10. KALAHARI
11. RESERVOIRS
12. POPULATION

Bonus: TRANSVAAL

World Geography Puzzles: Countries of the World — Answer Keys

Iraq Crossword Puzzle (p. 32)

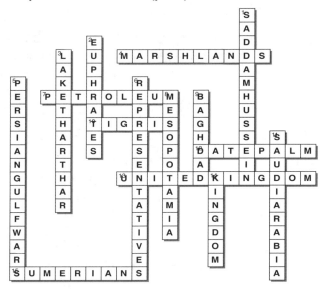

Japan Hidden Message Puzzle (p. 38)
1. J<u>A</u>PANESE <u>A</u>LPS
2. <u>I</u>SLANDS
3. HOKKAI<u>D</u>O
4. T<u>O</u>KYO
5. TECTONI<u>C</u>
6. <u>V</u>OLCANOES
7. TSUNAM<u>I</u>
8. HUR<u>R</u>ICANES
9. EMP<u>E</u>ROR
10. MAJORI<u>T</u>Y

Hidden Message: RADIOACTIVE

Australia Last Letter/First Letter Puzzle (pg. 40)
1. MURRUMBIDGEE
2. EYRE
3. EUROPEANS
4. SYDNEY HARBOR
5. RIVER SYSTEM
6. MALNUTRITION
7. NEW SOUTH WALES
8. SOUTH AUSTRALIA
9. ARTESIAN
10. NORTHEAST
11. TRADED
12. DIVIDING
13. GREAT VICTORIA
14. AUSTRALIA
15. ABORIGINES

India Word Scramble (p. 34)
1. SUBCONTINENT
2. HIMALAYA
3. KANGCHENJUNGA
4. INDO-GANGETIC
5. BRAHMAPUTRA
6. BENGAL
7. ARABIAN
8. WESTERN GHATS
9. AGRICULTURE
10. TECHNOLOGY
11. PAKISTAN
12. POVERTY

China Word Search Puzzle (p. 36)

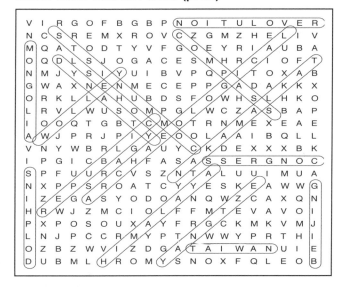

1. COMPASS
2. DYNASTY
3. REVOLUTION
4. REPUBLIC
5. COMMUNISTS
6. TAIWAN
7. BEIJING
8. CONGRESS
9. HIMALAYA
10. TAKAMAKAN
11. MONGOLIA
12. YANGTZE
13. YELLOW
14. ARCHAEOLOGICAL
15. DOLPHINS

BIBLIOGRAPHY

"11 Basic Facts About Canadians, General Info." *Live & Learn, An online community for new Manitobans.* 8 Jun. 2015. English Online Inc. 2 Feb. 2017. <https://livelearn.ca/article/about-canada/10-basic-things-to-know-about-canada/>

"About Croatia, Geography." *Study in Croatia.* 2010. Study in Croatia. 16 Feb. 2017. < http://www.studyincroatia.hr/about-croatia/geography>

"About Iraq, Geography." *Embassy of the Republic of Iraq. Public Relations Office.* 2005–2017. Embassy of the Republic of Iraq. 27 Feb. 2017. <http://www.iraqiembassy.us/page/geography>

"About Mexico, Geography." 2009. *AllAboutMexico.com.* Mexico Live, S.A. de C.V. 6 Feb. 2017 <http://www.allaboutmexico.com/geography.html>

"About Mexico, People." 2009. *AllAboutMexico.com.* Mexico Live, S.A. de C.V. 6 Feb. 2017 <http://www.allaboutmexico.com/people.html>

Barrow, Mandy. *Project Britain.* 2014. Mandy Barrow. 14 Feb. 2017. <http://www.projectbritain.com>

Barrow, Mandy. "Rivers, UK Rivers." *Primary Homework Help.* 2013. Mandy Barrow. 14 Feb. 2017. <http://www.primaryhomeworkhelp.co.uk/rivers/UK.htm>

"Building the Panama Canal, 1903–1914." Milestones: 1899–1913. 1 Nov. 2013. *Office of the Historian, Bureau of Public Affairs.* United States Department of State. 7 Feb. 2017. <https://history.state.gov/milestones/1899-1913/panama-canal>

"Canada's Five Regions, General Info." *Live & Learn, An online community for new Manitobans.* 27 Jun. 2016. English Online Inc. 2 Feb. 2017. <https://livelearn.ca/article/about-canada/canadas-five-regions/>

"Chile." *geographia.com.* 2010. interKnowledge Corp. 9 Feb. 2017. <http://geographia.com/chile/>

"France Rivers Map." *About-France.com.* 2003–2017. About-France.com. 15 Feb. 2017. <http://about-france.com/geo/france-rivers-map.htm>

"The Geography of Italy." *Understanding Italy.* 2010. Understanding Italy. 16 Feb. 2017. <http://www.understandingitaly.com/profile-content/geography.html>

"Iraq Facts." *National Geographic Travel.* 2015–2017. National Geographic Partners, LLC. 27 Feb. 2017. <http://travel.nationalgeographic.com/travel/countries/iraq-facts/>

"Italy". *Encyclopædia Britannica.* Encyclopædia Britannica Online. Encyclopædia Britannica Inc., 2017. Web. 17 Feb. 2017 <https://www.britannica.com/place/Italy>.

Meditz, Sandra W. and Hanratty, Dennis M., editors. "Geography." *Panama: A Country Study.* Washington: GPO for the Library of Congress, 1987. 7 Feb. 2017. <http://countrystudies.us/panama/24.htm>

Bibliography (cont.)

Meyer, Amelia. "Brazil." *www.brazil.org.za.* 2010. 8 Feb. 2017. <http://www.brazil.org.za/index.html>

National Geographic Kids. 2016. National Geographic Partners, LLC. Feb. 2017. <http://kids.nationalgeographic.com> (Accessed each available country's profile in the *National Geographic Kids* website.)

Nelson, Ken. "Geography for Kids: Australia." *Ducksters.* Mar. 2017. Technological Solutions, Inc. (TSI). 3 Mar. 2017. <http://www.ducksters.com/geography/country/australia.php>.

Nelson, Ken. "Geography for Kids: China." *Ducksters.* Feb. 2017. Technological Solutions, Inc. (TSI). 28 Feb. 2017. <http://www.ducksters.com/geography/country/china.php>

Nelson, Ken. "Geography for Kids: Egypt." *Ducksters.* Feb. 2017. Technological Solutions, Inc. (TSI). 21 Feb. 2017. < http://www.ducksters.com/geography/country/egypt.php>

Nelson, Ken. "Geography for Kids: Japan." *Ducksters.* Mar. 2017. Technological Solutions, Inc. (TSI). 2 Mar. 2017. <http://www.ducksters.com/geography/country/japan.php>

Nelson, Ken. "Kids History: Geography of Ancient China." *Ducksters.* Feb. 2017. Technological Solutions, Inc. (TSI). 28 Feb. 2017. <http://www.ducksters.com/history/china/geography_of_ancient_china.php>

Peel, Tony and Boo. "The Zambezi River." *Victoria Falls Guide.* 2017. Tony and Boo Peel. 23 Feb. 2017. < http://www.victoriafalls-guide.net/zambezi-river.html>

"Russia Geography." *Maps of World.* 2002–2017 Compare Infobase Ltd. MapXL. 20 Feb. 2017. <http://www.mapsofworld.com/russia/geography/>

Schultz, Alarich R., Crist, Raymond E., and others (contributors). "Hydrology, Amazon River." *Encyclopædia Britannica.* Encyclopædia Britannica Online. 24 Sept. 2009. Encyclopædia Britannica Inc. 8 Feb. 2017. <https://www.britannica.com/place/Amazon-River/Hydrology>

"Wildlife." *Zambia.* 2017. Zambia Tourism. 23 Feb. 2017. < http://www.zambiatourism.com/about-zambia/wildlife>

worldatlas.com. Valnet Inc, 2016. Feb. 2017. <http://www.worldatlas.com> (Accessed each available country's profile on the *worldatlas.com* website.)

The World Factbook 2013–14. Central Intelligence Agency. 2013. Washington, DC: Central Intelligence Agency. Feb. 2017. <https://www.cia.gov/library/publications/the-world-factbook/index.html> (Accessed each country's profile on *The World Factbook* website.)

WORLD GEOGRAPHY PUZZLES: COUNTRIES OF THE WORLD PHOTO CREDITS

All photos found at <https://commons.wikimedia.org/wiki/File:...>. File name is listed in each credit.

pg. 1   Parliament Ottawa River.jpg {{PD-GFDL/CC-SA-3.0}} Adam the atom. 26 May 2006.

pg. 2   10seppalasleddogs.jpg {{PD-GFDL/CC-SA-3.0}} Isa Boucher, The Seppala Siberian Sleddog Project. c. 1994. ToB. 24 May 2005.

pg. 2   Hwy 5 to Inuvik - the Dempster Hwy, (5856972137).jpg {{PD-CC-SA-2.0}} Murray Foubister (Https://www.flickr.com/people/61456446@N05). 1 Jun. 2010. Fæ. 27 Sept. 2016.

pg. 2   Lake Kinney mit Mount Whitehorn.jpg {{PD-CC-SA-3.0}} Florian Fuchs. 19 Aug. 2012.

pg. 2   Confederation Bridge from Prince Edward island 16x9.jpg {{PD-Author/CC-SA-3.0}} WikiPedant at Wikimedia Commons. 20 Aug. 2007.

pg. 2   Newglasgowpano2.jpg {{PD-GFDL/CC-SA-3.0}} Chensiyuan at the English language Wikipedia. 24 Jul. 2006.

pg. 3   Palacio de Bellas Artes.jpg {{PD-CC-SA-2.0}} Carolina López (http://flickr.com/photos/98553744@N00). 25 May 2007.

pg. 4   Cascada Basaseachi.jpg {{PD-GFDL/CC-SA-2.5}} Err0neous at English Wikipedia. 15 Jul. 2006. Angusmclellan. 18 Mar. 2007.

pg. 4   Acapulco - Visto desde la Capilla Ecuménica de la Paz.JPG {{PD-GFDL/CC-SA-2.0}} Mitrush. 19 Feb. 2006. Sealight. 19 Aug. 2008.

pg. 5   Panama Canal Gatun Locks.jpg {{PD-GFDL/CC-SA-3.0}} Stan Shebs. 2 Jan. 2000.

pg. 6   Panamá - panoramio (5).jpg {{PD-CC-SA-3.0}} Octavio Cogley. 13 Feb. 2009. Panoramio upload. 14 Dec. 2016.

pg. 6   Panama City (26898155830).jpg {{PD-CC-SA-2.0}} dronepier (https://www.flickr.com/people/132646954@N02). 21 Mar. 2016

pg. 7   Senado2006.jpg {{PD-CC-SA-3.0}} Wilson Dias/ABR. 17 Oct. 2006. Dantadd. 18 Oct. 2006.

pg. 8   Ararasmatogrossodosul02.JPG {{PD-CC-SA-4.0}} Ranantondin. 22 Oct. 2014.

pg. 8   Amazonas, Brasilien (11672038173).jpg {{PD-CC-SA-2.0}} M M (https://www.flickr.com/people/43423301@N07). from Switzerland. 29 Dec. 2013. The Photographer. 28 May 2015.

pg. 8   Pico da Neblina.jpg {PD-CC-SA-3.0}} Robson Esteves Czaban (http://www.birding.com.br/Portugues/FotografiadeAves.htm). 1998. Chronus. 27 Jun. 2010.

pg. 9   Chuquicamata-003.jpg {{PD-GFDL/CC-SA-3.0}} Reinhard Jahn. Mar. 1984. Nanosmile. 2 Oct. 2005.

pg. 10 Moai Rano raraku.jpg {PD-Author}} Aurbina at English Wikipedia. Jan 2004. Kahusi. 7 May 2005.

pg. 11 Atlantic V, Grundsund.JPG {{PD-CC-SA-4.0}} I99pema. 3 Jul. 2015

pg. 11. Reindeer herding.jpg {{PD-CC-SA-2.0}} Mats Andersson (http://www.flickr.com/photos/51496968@N00)

pg. 12 Kebnekaise-1.jpg {{PD-Author}} SiriusA. 7 Feb. 2008.

pg. 12 Runebomme or Sami drum 01.jpg {{PD-CC-SA-2.0}} Åge Hojem. NTNU University Museum (https://www.flickr.com/photos/vitenskapsmuseet/19288847594) 12 May 2015. ThereseRS. 14 Oct. 2015.

pg. 12 Coat of arms Dronprins Carl Gustav av Sverige.svg {PD-CC-SA-3.0}} Wikibelgiaan. 29 Nov. 2013.

pg. 13 House.of.parliament.overall.arp.jpg {{PD-Author}} Adrian Pingstone. Jun. 2006.

pg. 14 Ardglass (2), May 2009.JPG {{PD-CC-SA-3.0}} Ardfern. 30 May 2009.

pg. 14 Ben Nevis - geograph.org.uk - 614456.jpg {{PD-CC-SA-2.0}} wfmillar (http://www.geograph.org.uk/profile/7544). 27 Apr. 1995. GeographBot. 7 Feb. 2011.

pg. 15 Sancerre vu depuis Chavignol.jpg {{PD-CC-SA-4.0}} Cjp24. 22 Oct. 2016.

pg. 16 Eiffel Tower from north Avenue de New York, Aug 2010.jpg {{PD-CC-SA-3.0}} Julie Anne Workman. 21 Aug. 2010.

pg. 16 Beaulieu-BaiDesFourmisC-20071102.jpg {{PD-Author}} Patrice Semeria. 2 Sept. 2007. Agora1950. 4 Nov. 2007.

pg. 17 King Tomislav Art Pavillon Zagreb.JPG {{PD-CC-SA-3.0}} Zeitblick. 9 Jul. 2013.

pg. 18 Dubrovnik june 2011.JPG {{PD-CC-SA-3.0}} Bracodbk. 21 Jun. 2011.

pg. 18 Ilok 001.jpg {PD-CC-SA-2.5}} Goran.Smith2-commonwiki. 25 Dec. 2006.

pg. 19 Venise la Piéta et campanile des Greci.JPG {{PD-CC-SA-3.0}} Alainauzas. 28 Apr. 2013.